K·I·S·S

DK

The Only Guides You'll Ever Need!

THIS SERIES IS YOUR TRUSTED GUIDE through all of life's stages and situations. Want to learn how to surf the Internet or care for your new puppy? Or maybe you'd like to become a wine connoisseur or an expert gardener? The solution is simple: Just pick up a K.I.S.S. Guide and turn to the first page.

Expert authors will walk you through the subject from start to finish, using simple blocks of knowledge to build your skills one step at a time. Build upon these learning blocks and by the end of the book, you'll be an expert yourself! Or, if you are familiar with the topic but want to learn more, it's easy to dive in and pick up where you left off.

The K.I.S.S. Guides deliver what they promise: simple access to all the information you'll need on one subject. Other titles you might want to check out include: Golf, Weight Loss, Pregnancy, Feng Shui, Massage, and many more to come.

K·I·S·S

GUIDE TO RAISING A

Puppy

LIZ PALIKA

Foreword by Alan Gomberg
Associate Editor, *American Kennel Club Gazette*

DK Publishing

LONDON, NEW YORK, MUNICH,
MELBOURNE, DELHI

DK Publishing, Inc.

Editor Beth Adelman
Series Editor Jennifer Williams
Editorial Director Chuck Wills

Dorling Kindersley Limited

Project Editor Julian Gray
Project Art Editor Martin Dieguez

Managing Editor Maxine Lewis
Managing Art Editor Heather McCarry
Production Heather Hughes
Picture Researcher Samantha Nunn
Category Publisher Mary Thompson

Dorling Kindersley India Limited

Project Editor Ranjana Saklani
Project Art Editor Aparna Sharma
Designer Rashmi Battoo
DTP Designer Sunil Sharma

Copyright © 2002
Dorling Kindersley Limited
Text copyright © 2002 Liz Palika
02 03 04 05 06 07 10 9 8 7 6 5 4 3 2 1

Published in the United States by
DK Publishing, Inc., 375 Hudson Street, New York, NY 10016

Palika, Liz, 1954-
    KISS guide to raising a puppy / Liz Palika.-- 1st American ed.
        p. cm. -- (Keep it simple series)
    ISBN 0-7894-8947-3 (alk. paper)
    1. Puppies. I. Title: KISS guide to raising a puppy. II. Title: Guide to raising a puppy.
III. Title. IV. Series.

SF426 .P325 2002
636.7'07--dc21

                                                                            2001058418

Color reproduction by ColourScan, Singapore
Printed and bound by MOHN media and Mohndruck GmbH, Germany

For our complete catalogue visit

www.dk.com

Contents at a Glance

CONTENTS

Foreword

OF ALL NON-HUMAN SPECIES, *the dog seems to be the one that is most devoted to us. Dogs are complex creatures. Each is a unique and unpredictable entity. That is part of the fascination they hold for us. Although many other species have strong personalities, it does seem as if dogs' personalities are stronger, more fascinating, more . . . well . . . nearly human. Or does it just seem that way because of the closeness that exists between dogs and people? Do we understand dogs in a way that we don't understand any other species? Almost everyone seems to agree that cats are ultimately mysterious, but dogs are not, or at least much less so. Something seems to happen between people and dogs that does not happen between people and any other species.*

Despite this closeness, this special empathy between people and dogs, you are not taking in an extension of yourself when you welcome a dog into your life and home. A dog's love and loyalty has to be earned. Some degree of work on your part is involved. And even though it sometimes seems as if your dog really understands you, you still can't talk to a dog. Or at least telling your dog not to bark for hours every time you go out or not to chew your slippers won't do any good. There are ways, though, to communicate with your dog and, when necessary, change your dog's behavior.

These are some of the reasons why educating yourself is so important, even before you choose a dog. You owe this to both yourself and the dog. If this new partnership is to be successful, you will have to work at bonding with and training your dog. With some breeds, this is easier than with others. And some breeds will be more suitable for you than others. Learning which breeds are right for you (and which are not) is essential.

But that's just the beginning. Not that you need to know everything before you start. You couldn't, anyway, because every dog is different, and some things can only be learned through experience. But having a guide can make a big difference – a simple, step-by-step guide, to see you through the beginning and other times that may be rough, to give you the basic information clearly, and to direct you to where you can find more info when you need it.

I can think of no better person to guide you than Liz Palika. Liz is in every way an advocate for the welfare of dogs. Part of this advocacy is reflected in her work as a trainer, helping dog owners learn how to live happily with their dogs. Another part can be seen in her work with homeless animals of several types, not just dogs. Liz's experience, her combination of knowledge and common sense, and her ability to communicate what you need to know – these make her a great helper for you and your canine pal.

In this book, Liz covers a tremendous amount, clearly and concisely. If you need a basic, practical guide to help you in the human–canine adventure, you have it here.

ALAN GOMBERG
ASSOCIATE EDITOR
AMERICAN KENNEL CLUB GAZETTE

Introduction

I HAVE BEEN TEACHING dog training classes for more than 20 years, and throughout that time people have asked me the same questions over and over. Many of these questions are directly related to puppy behavior:
- Why does my puppy nip me?
- Why is he digging up my backyard?
- My neighbours say he barks when I'm not home. What can I do?

Other questions have to do with training:
- Why does my puppy fight the leash?
- Why doesn't she come when I call her?
- How can I stop her from dashing through every open door?

Many puppy owners also have questions about how to care for their puppy:
- Which vaccinations should my puppy get and when?
- Can I feed her generic puppy food? It's much cheaper!
- How can I clean her ears? How often should I bathe her?

In the KISS Guide to Raising a Puppy I have compiled all the answers to the thousands of questions that puppy owners have asked me throughout the years. I am a firm believer in the adage, "There is no such thing as a stupid question." If it was important enough for you to ask, then the answer is just as important!

I really want you to enjoy your puppy. And that means understanding him, training him, taking good care of him, and doing things with him. I know puppies can be a handful, but when you understand why they do things, and know how to teach them what the limits are, you'll both have a much happier time together.

Since this book is for everyone who loves dogs, it is written so everyone can understand it. If you are an experienced dog owner, don't take offence at the basic material you may think everyone knows. Everyone doesn't! But keep reading, because there is information here for everyone.

I'll begin by helping you decide what type of dog will be right for you. Then we'll talk about what to do on your puppy's first day home. We'll look at housetraining, basic obedience training, and I'll also tell you how you can use training and some ingenuity to solve most of the problems puppies get into.

I'll look at many aspects of your puppy's health. I'll give you advice on how to choose a vet, and tell you when your puppy should be seeing the doc. And, although I hope you'll never need it, I'll tell you what to do in an emergency. I'll also let you know about some of the fun things you can do with a puppy.

As always, I have to thank my husband Paul for his patience – his never-ending patience! When he comes home from work and I tell him, "Guess what? That vacation we were talking about is on hold again. I have a book contract," he just shakes his head, asks me if I have enough time and sighs. He sighs a lot! I don't think he had any idea what he was getting into when he married me 24 years ago. Thank you, Paul!

Thanks, too, to the Kelley family – Ed, Denys, Sarah, and Katie – who helped with puppy classes, and with this book. Thanks all! I must also thank my sister, Mary, and my good friends, Petra and Kerry. They have taken over teaching my classes when I'm too busy writing or when I'm off to a dog show. They have helped me with book signings, photo shots, and all of my dog-related activities. Thanks again; I couldn't do it without you!

Liz Palika

LIZ PALIKA

What's Inside?

THE INFORMATION IN the K.I.S.S. Guide to Raising a Puppy *is arranged to keep in step with you and your questions, as your puppy grows up. At the same time, important tips are repeated whenever necessary, so you're never left guessing.*

PART ONE

In Part One I discuss the things you should think about even before you get a puppy: Can you invest the time and money and can you make the required changes to your home and lifestyle? If yes, I go on to help you choose the puppy that'll be best for you.

PART TWO

In Part Two I discuss in detail the preparations you have to make before you bring your puppy home and the care you should take immediately after he comes home. I also show you how you can immediately start housetraining and socialization.

PART THREE

Part Three will teach you how to maintain your puppy's health beginning with your pup's first visit to the vet. Then, I'll take you through vaccination, puppy food, exercise, bathing, grooming, and parasites. I'll also teach you first-aid and what to do in an emergency.

PART FOUR

In Part Four I focus on dog training and how it's something you and your puppy do together. We discuss what tools you should use for training, when you should be patient or strict, and how you can keep it fun and easy for both of you. You can also learn how to discourage problem behaviour.

PART FIVE

Part Five tells you that games are fun and can be good exercise as well as a great way to spend time with your puppy. I'll give you some good suggestions of games you can play with your puppy. I'll also try to solve some puzzles of canine behaviour for you, such as, "Why is she willing to eat garbage on the street when she's so picky about the food at home?"

The Extras

THROUGHOUT THE BOOK *you'll notice a number of boxes and icons.*
These are meant to emphasise certain points that I want to be sure you pay
attention to. They'll help you really understand what I'm talking about.
Look for:

Very Important Point

This icon will point
out a bit of information
I believe deserves your
careful attention. You
really need to know this
before continuing.

Complete No-No

This is a warning
symbol, pointing
out something I
want to advise you
not to do.

Getting Technical

Here I will let
you know that the
information might get
a bit technical, so you'll
need to read carefully.

Inside Scoop

These are special
suggestions that
come from my own
personal experience.
I want to share them
with you because
these tips helped me when
I was learning about puppies.

In the margins you'll also find additional
information that I think you will enjoy or
find helpful. Look for:

Trivia...

These are simply fun facts
that will give you an extra
appreciation for the
uniqueness of puppies and
their place in our world.

DEFINITION

Don't speak dog? I'll define all
*those **doggy words** for you,*
whenever they occur in the
book. Also, there's a Glossary
at the back of the book with
all the canine lingo.

INTERNET

www.dk.com

There's a lot of great
information available on the
web, and I will be pointing
out relevant web sites that
will add to your enjoyment
and understanding of dogs.

PART ONE

Chapter 1

Are You Ready For a Puppy?

PUPPIES ARE SO ADORABLE that it's hard not to want one. However, don't decide to bring one home on impulse. Evaluate the time and financial obligations involved and consult your family because they'll live with the puppy. Think before you add this 12- to 14-year commitment to your life.

In this chapter:

✓ How busy are you?

✓ Where do you live?

✓ Who will live with the puppy?

✓ Can you afford a puppy?

✓ Will you enjoy life with a puppy?

✓ There are good points to puppy ownership

How busy are you?

A PUPPY WILL REQUIRE a substantial time commitment from you. In the first few days after being taken away from his mom and littermates, a puppy will be lonely and possibly afraid. You (and other family members) will need to spend time with the puppy to reassure him that he is loved and safe. If you can bring the puppy home on a Friday night and spend most of the weekend with him, that would be perfect.

Time for bonding

Bonding with the puppy also takes time. This time is well spent, because it is this bond that makes dog ownership so special. Often, puppy owners tell me that their new puppy prefers to spend time with their old dog rather than with the family. What happened was that the new puppy spent more time with the older dog, and as a result, bonded more strongly with him.

To make sure your puppy bonds strongly with you and not your older dog, your neighbor, or the cat, for the first few weeks after you bring home a puppy you will need to spend a lot of time with him.

Time to train

You will also need time to start teaching your puppy. Housetraining, of course, is a necessity and it certainly takes time. Teaching your puppy other household rules, such as what to chew on (and what not to chew on) also takes time. An early start in basic obedience commands such as "sit," "walk on a leash," and "come," are important to ensure good behavior later. Moreover, you will want to enroll yourself and your puppy in a puppy kindergarten training class, and will have homework to practice from class. All of this takes time.

■ **Start training your puppy** *as soon as you bring him home, especially with regard to his toilet habits.*

Time for grooming

You will also need to schedule time for daily grooming sessions, including brushing, combing, and flea and tick control. Weekly grooming sessions are needed for bathing the puppy and trimming toenails. Some breeds require more grooming than others. For example, a long, fuzzy Bouvier des Flandres puppy will need a good half-hour grooming session each day – minimum! But all puppies need the basics.

Time for exercise

In the beginning, play times will be simple and short, but as your puppy grows, his stamina and endurance will increase, and his exercise needs will increase as well.

You must allot time for exercise. Many canine behavior problems result from too much energy and not enough exercise.

Time for everything else

As your puppy grows up, you will need to rethink your time with him. You won't need to spend time housetraining because (hopefully!) he will be well housetrained. He will also understand the household rules and will be well behaved when left alone. But you may want to teach him something else. How about dog games or activities, like frisbee, flyball, or how to do tricks? You may also decide to get involved in therapy dog volunteer work. All of these activities, which are great for you and your puppy, take time.

■ **Even if you decide** *not to do anything beyond basic training with your puppy, he'll still always need training reviews, exercise time, walks, grooming, play sessions, and just plain old love!*

Where do you live?

DOGS CAN LIVE just about anywhere. They are infinitely adaptable creatures. However, some situations will require more work or more ingenuity from you. If you want a puppy, you can make it work.

What will the neighbors say?

What will your neighbors say when you bring home a dog? You may think it's none of their business, but they can make life very difficult for you, your family, and your dog if they are unhappy with the situation. Sometimes it helps to prepare a neighbor ahead of time. Ask your neighbors what their favorite breeds of dog are, what good memories they have of dogs, and mention that you are thinking about getting one. Ask if they know of a good dog trainer. Let your neighbors know that you want to make sure your new dog won't be a problem. My grandma said, "You can catch more flies with honey than you can with vinegar." Dealing with neighbors sometimes requires a great deal of honey!

Trivia...

More neighbors complain about excessive barking than any other factor related to dog ownership. Boredom, too much time alone, and not enough exercise or training can contribute to barking, but some breeds are more prone to barking than others. They include Beagles, Cocker Spaniels, German Shepherds, Pomeranians, Poodles, Shetland Sheepdogs, and Siberian Huskies.

Do you have the space?

How big is your home? Although many large dogs are not as active as smaller ones, they do take up physical space. If a St. Bernard is sprawled across your living room floor, will you still have room to walk? Do you have room for the puppy, his bed, toys, bowls, grooming supplies, and other necessities of puppy life?

■ **A well-decorated house** *and beautiful furnishings do not go with a livewire young puppy.*

Do you have the patience?

Your puppy will have housetraining accidents, spill his food, slobber water all over the floor, and track dirt in from outside. He will come in from playing in the rain and shake dirty water all over.

He will bring you – as a gift – a dirty stick with dead leaves and may also bring a pinecone covered in mud and sticky with sap, or a very dead, decomposing mouse, not to make you angry but to share it with you. He will inevitably break things – not intentionally, of course. Things will get chewed on and knocked down. Dogs' tails have been known to clear a coffee table in one swipe. It's amazing how powerful even a puppy's tail can be!

Puppies make a mess – it's that simple!

DO YOU HAVE A YARD?

A securely fenced yard does make puppy ownership easier:

1 Housetraining is easier with a yard. Once the puppy recognizes the area in the yard where you train him to relieve himself, he will not have accidents inside.

2 With a secure yard, you can let the puppy play outside when you need time alone.

However, apartment dwellers can still have a puppy. It will just take more time, a consistent routine, and more effort on your part.

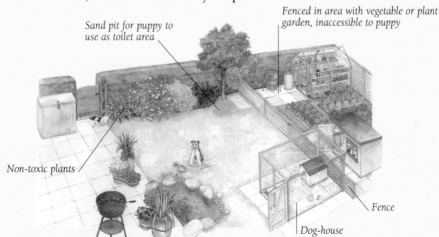

Sand pit for puppy to use as toilet area

Fenced in area with vegetable or plant garden, inaccessible to puppy

Non-toxic plants

Fence

Dog-house

■ **A nice yard** *with precious flowers and a young puppy can easily co-exist. Simply fence off a certain portion of the yard for him. You could make a dog-run and let the puppy have free access to that area, or even build a dog-house for him as a kind of "home right outside home."*

It's the law

If you rent your home, will your landlord allow you to keep a dog?

In most states it is legal for landlords to forbid pet ownership. They can also limit ownership to dogs of a certain size or weight, or limit the number of pets you may have. Home ownership associations can do the same.

Many communities also have laws concerning dog ownership. Some cities and counties have enacted breed-specific laws that make ownership of certain breeds illegal. Rottweilers, Pit Bulls, and German Shepherds have been the targets of such laws. It may seem strange to condemn an entire breed because of one or two incidents, but it happens. Make sure you know the laws of your community before you get a puppy.

Who will live with the puppy?

DOES EVERYONE IN THE FAMILY *want this new puppy? If some family members or roommates are less than pleased at the prospect of a puppy, the dog will suffer for it. One person's animosity, lack of caring, anger, neglect, or abuse could severely traumatize the puppy – an experience you should not subject this vulnerable creature to. Everyone must be in agreement before you bring your puppy home.*

The kids

Are there young children in your family? Often the parents of young children get a puppy so that the dog and kids can grow up together. This is fine, as long as you remember that a young puppy often looks at a young child as an equal and will play with the child as he does with another puppy. That means he will chase, jump on, and grab the child with his teeth, which can scare and hurt the child. Parents must be ready to supervise playtimes and make sure the puppy never takes advantage.

■ **Take care** *that the puppy doesn't hurt your child while playing with him.*

The older folks

Will this puppy be living with a senior citizen? A puppy can add a lot of joy and laughter to a senior's life, as long as the senior citizen is able to deal with the energy level of a puppy. Many seniors also hesitate to discipline a puppy, even when the discipline is well deserved. They tell me, "I've raised my family; now I just want a friend and companion." In these situations, sometimes it's better if the senior adopts an adult dog rather than a puppy. However, if the senior citizen is healthy, active, and able to do what is needed for a puppy, well then, go for it!

Many widows and widowers get a new puppy after losing their spouse. A dog gives them something to care for, love, and shower with affection. A dog also relieves the terrible loneliness the surviving spouse feels after losing a loved one.

■ **Consider your age,** *as well as health and energy levels, before you get yourself a puppy.*

Single people

Do you live alone? Many single adults own dogs, and although this situation can work very well, it does require dedication from the dog owner. In a two-adult household (with or without kids) there is more than one person to care for the puppy and spend time with him. However, in a single-person home, that person is responsible for everything. This takes some dedication.

If you live alone, work long hours (9 hours or more each day), and spend a great deal of time away from home, don't get a puppy.

However, if you work from home or work close to home and can spend time with the puppy, great! He will be a wonderful companion for you.

Other pets

Will this new puppy be coming into a household where there are already other pets? If you have a dog or two, adding a puppy will probably be very easy; you've done this before and know what to expect. In addition, your dogs are already socialized to other dogs, so problems should be minimal. However, if you are adding a puppy to a house with resident cats, problems could (and probably will) ensue. Make sure you are willing to spend the time and effort to teach everyone how to get along.

Can you afford a puppy?

BUYING A PUPPY *from a breeder or adopting one from the local humane society is only the first financial obligation your puppy will incur.*

For the first year of your puppy's life, it will seem as if your money is disappearing into one of those black holes astronomers talk about.

Puppy supplies

Your puppy will need supplies – a leash and collar, a bed or kennel crate, toys and chewies, and good food – all of which cost money. He will need several vaccinations and will need to be checked over by a veterinarian to make sure he's healthy. When he's old enough, he will need to be neutered (the females will be spayed). He will also need to be licensed. You may have to spend some money to shore up your backyard fence to make sure it's puppy-proof. Or you may want to build a dog run so that you can protect your backyard. Many dog owners wish they had invested in their local home building center's stock before getting their puppy!

Medical emergencies

In addition, you will need to be ready for emergencies. What happens if your puppy cuts himself and needs stitches? Or gets stung by a bee and has an allergic reaction? Off to the veterinarian you go, checkbook in hand! Puppies do cost money – not just to buy, but to maintain. You need to be aware of all the potential costs before bringing home the puppy, because it isn't fair to deny the puppy proper care just because you didn't realize earlier how much it would cost.

■ **Vets are necessary** *not only in medical crises, but also for vaccinations, periodic check-ups, and advice on any special care that your puppy may need. These essential services will cost you money.*

Will you enjoy living with a puppy?

MANY POTENTIAL DOG OWNERS *don't realize how much a puppy will change their lifestyle. A new puppy isn't like a new houseplant; you can't add it to your home and expect everything else to remain the same. A new puppy will require you to change some things.*

Heading off trouble

You will have to be more aware of objects, since puppies love to chew. You won't be able to leave your shoes in the middle of the floor; you'll have to put them away. You will have to close doors behind you, close closet doors, and put up barriers to keep the puppy out of trouble.

■ **Be careful** *where you put your possessions – chewing is a young puppy's favorite activity!*

You will have to puppy-proof your house and put away the valuables that you don't want him to break. You will also have to watch him to make sure he doesn't get into trouble. A puppy will require you to spend time with him, be aware of him, and be watchful.

Control your temper

You will also have to be forgiving. If your puppy chews on your shoes because you left them in the middle of the floor, it's not his fault. It's your fault for leaving them there. Yes, you can say "no" when you take the shoes away, but don't scold him any more than that. Next time, make sure you don't leave the shoes there. The same thing applies to housetraining. If your puppy asks to go outside and you are too busy or don't pay attention, you cannot scold the puppy for the resulting puddle. It's your job to pay attention, especially when a puppy is involved. An older dog will have better bladder control and will often wait until he can get your attention, but when a puppy needs to go outside, he needs to go now!

A puppy is a wonderful addition to your life if you are aware of the changes it will make and if you are ready to make those changes.

Trivia...

In 1903, the famous sports cartoonist Tad Dorgan made a drawing of a sausage in a roll, drawing the sausage like a Dachshund. That's where we get the term "hot dog."

There are good points to puppy ownership

SO FAR I HAVE DISCUSSED *many of the negative aspects of puppy ownership. But puppyhood is certainly not all hard work, messes, and money. There are lots of great things about having a puppy.*

INTERNET

www.canismajor.com/
dog/guide

This page has a wide variety of articles about puppies and dogs, and links to even more.

They're cute!

Puppies are cute. I don't think there is anything quite as cute as an 8 week-old puppy. That round, full belly with a leg at each corner is adorable. How can you not love the wet tongue, fuzzy coat, floppy paws, soft ears, and wagging tail that quivers at your every word? What about puppy breath? There is nothing in the world like the milky smell of puppy's breath. Some people like the smell of a (human) baby's head, while other people love the smell of a new car. Me, I love puppy breath!

Everyone loves them

A puppy is also a way of touching other people. When you take a puppy (and later, a dog) for a walk, you will find yourself talking to your neighbors, meeting new people and having fun with the neighborhood kids. People like dogs and will talk to you about your dog.

They're funny

We've known for years that laughter makes us feel better, and now even health care professionals are telling us that laughter is genuinely good for us. A puppy will also make you laugh, and that's good medicine! For him everything is a toy to be chewed on, growled at, and shaken to death. While doing all this, the puppy is adorably clumsy and uncoordinated, tripping over his own feet.

■ **Watching puppies play** *is great fun and can do you a world of good.*

They're fascinating

I also feel a sense of wonder about the world around me when I'm watching a puppy. It's easy in our busy world to forget to look around and really see what's happening. But to a young puppy, everything is new and exciting. When watching a puppy discover the world – investigate a grasshopper, chase a butterfly, or smell a flower – you can renew your own sense of wonder. What a wonderful world we live in!

When I get a new puppy I always fall in love with him, but I am also thinking of the adult dog that he will become and our future together. Will we go camping and explore new places? Will we train in a new dog sport? Will this puppy be like Ursa and wash my face when I cry at a movie? Will he be like Dax and bring me toys when he wants attention? I look forward to the new relationship we will forge together, because this new puppy will become my new best friend. What a promise of things to come!

SLEEPING BEAUTIES

A simple summary

✔ Puppies require a great deal of time. If you want to get a puppy, you will need to set aside that kind of time.

✔ Before you get a puppy, look at your living situation and make sure a puppy will fit in.

✔ Everyone in the household must want the puppy and be able to handle it.

✔ A puppy is a financial obligation; make sure you can afford to give him the care he needs.

✔ You will get unconditional love from your puppy, but he'll also mess up the house and disrupt routine. Can you deal with that?

✔ Your puppy will bring laughter, joy, and wonder, and on growing up will become your best friend.

Chapter 2

Big or Small, Longhaired or Short?

THERE ARE MORE THAN 400 DOG BREEDS recognised worldwide. This single species, *Canis Familiaris*, is made up of more varied and diverse breeds than any other: Tiny dogs, no more than 2lb (900g) and gigantic ones more than 200lb (91kg); dogs that herd sheep on grassy meadows; dogs that swim to retrieve waterfowl; and dogs that originated in desert lands. Some have long, silky, flowing coats; some have short, slick coats; others have coarse, curly coats. There are even dogs with no hair at all except little puffs on the head and legs. So which kind of dog do you want?

In this chapter:

✓ Long hair or short?

✓ Canine personalities

✓ The idea of breeds

Long hair or short?

COAT TYPES ARE PURELY *a personal preference. Some people like the look and feel of a short, slick coat, while others like to snuggle up to a furry, silky-coated friend. Make sure you'll be comfortable with the feel of a specific breed's coat, as well as the upkeep and grooming that particular coat will require.*

Mid-length coats

Coat types vary incredibly among breeds. Australian Shepherds and Collies have a medium-length, silky coat that is easy to brush and care for. It will rarely **mat** and dirt will fall out of it. However, these dogs do shed, and heavily so twice a year.

■ **Afghan Hounds** *evolved their thick, long coat against the bitter cold of the high mountains in Central Asia. However, this coat rapidly forms thick mats without grooming. Achieving such a well-groomed, elegant look, therefore, takes some dedicated caring.*

German Shepherds, also a herding breed, have a shorter outer coat (than Australian Shepherds or Collies), but they have a thick, heavy undercoat. A German Shepherd's coat never mats, but it sheds very heavily twice a year and a little bit all the time.

Short coats

Boxers (see below), Doberman Pinschers, Labrador Retrievers, Pointers, Smooth Fox Terriers, and Weimaraners have short, slick coats that aren't long enough to tangle or mat. However, don't make the mistake of thinking this short coat doesn't shed; it does, and twice a year these breeds shed heavily. The hair that is shed is short instead of long – just the right length for working its way into your sofa cushions.

■ **Boxers** *have a short, smooth, shiny coat that lies flat on their body. You can get by with grooming them once a week with a brush or a chamois.*

Long, flowing coats

The Irish, English, and Gordon Setters have a gorgeous long, flowing coat that is absolutely stunning, but this coat comes with a price. It needs to be combed daily or it will mat – and it is capable of matting horribly! Afghan Hounds (shown on opposite page) also have a long, silky coat that needs regular, thorough combing.

Coats that always grow

Many other breeds, including Poodles and Cocker Spaniels, have hair that grows constantly and needs regular grooming and haircuts. If you cannot cut the dog's hair yourself, make sure you take the cost of professional grooming into consideration before getting one of these breeds. As a general rule, most of these breeds should get a haircut or professional grooming every 4 to 6 weeks. In between, you will need to keep them combed, dematted, and brushed.

Grooming costs vary, depending upon the area where you live, the economy, and the breed of dog you have. However, as an average, grooming for a Cocker Spaniel will cost between $20 and $40. An Old English Sheepdog's shampoo, brush, comb, and haircut may run between $40 and $60.

Grooming prices go up if a dog is matted, has fleas, or is badly behaved. If you do not keep up the dog's coat, or if your dog is poorly trained, expect to pay more.

Breeds that need regular grooming and haircuts

- Airedale
- Bichon Frise
- Bouvier des Flandres
- English Cocker Spaniel
- English Springer Spaniel
- Lhasa Apso
- Maltese
- Old English Sheepdog
- Pekingese
- Pomeranian
- Toy, Miniature, and Standard Poodle
- Miniature, Standard, and Giant Schnauzer
- Scottish Terrier
- Shih Tzu
- Silky Terrier
- Welsh Springer Spaniel
- Welsh Terrier
- West Highland White Terrier
- Wire Fox Terrier
- Yorkshire Terrier (shown here)

■ **Yorkshire Terriers,** *one of the breeds with no undercoat, need sensitive handling. They also need to have their hair trimmed about once a month.*

Canine personalities

THERE IS NOTHING MORE ANNOYING to a calm, laid-back person than someone who is bouncing around, ready for activity at any moment. I know, because I am one of those couch potato people. However, one of my best friends (the human kind) is a high-energy, ready-to-go person. To maintain our friendship, I simply avoid her when I want some couch time. Dogs also have differences in personality and activity levels. Some breeds are known for being more active, while others are more laid back.

The key to a successful relationship is to match your personality and activity level with your canine.

Excitability

Excitability is usually referred to as the dog's ability to "come alive" when something happens, such as the doorbell ringing. Some breeds are more easily excited then others. The comparative lists given in the box (opposite) are a generalization, of course, because individual dogs have different levels of excitability.

Activity level

Excitability does not necessarily mean a breed also has a high activity level, although the two do often go hand in hand. A high activity level (see box) means this breed is more active, whether or not something specific is going on that might make a dog want to run around. Some owners – such as my active friend – prefer a dog that is more active, whereas I prefer a dog that is more relaxed, like me.

Desire to play

Most dog owners like to play with their dogs. People with a high energy level usually enjoy an active dog that likes to play a lot (check box for comparisons). A family with several children may need a dog that likes to play a lot, but a senior citizen with health problems might prefer a dog that is less active and less driven to play.

■ **Dachshunds** *were bred to have short limbs so that they could go into burrows after prey.*

CANINE COMPARISONS AT A GLANCE

The lists given below will help you choose the right puppy for you on the basis of the personality traits she will exhibit, not just as a puppy, but all her life.

Easily excited breeds

Chihuahua
Fox Terrier
Jack Russell Terrier
Scottish Terrier
Shih Tzu
Silky Terrier
West Highland White Terrier
Yorkshire Terrier

Calm breeds

Akita
Alaskan Malamute
Bloodhound
Bulldog
Chow Chow
Newfoundland
Rottweiler
St. Bernard

Active breeds

Border Collie
Cocker Spaniel
Smooth and Wire Fox Terrier
Jack Russell Terrier
Miniature Pinscher
Miniature Schnauzer
Pomeranian
Shetland Sheepdog
Shih Tzu
Silky Terrier
West Highland White Terrier

Laid-back breeds

Akita
Alaskan Malamute
Basset Hound
Bloodhound
Bulldog
Chow Chow
Golden Retriever
Great Dane
Newfoundland
Pug
St. Bernard

Breeds that need to play less

Australian Shepherd
Border Collie
English Springer Spaniel
German Shepherd
Golden Retriever
Irish Setter
Labrador Retriever
Toy, Miniature, and Standard Poodle
Shetland Sheepdog

Breeds that need to play more

Akita
Basset Hound
Bloodhound
Bulldog
Chihuahua
Dachshund
Greyhound
Pekingese
St. Bernard

Demand for affection

Some breeds crave being with their owner as much as possible. When these dogs are not with their owner, especially for hours at a time, behavior problems can result. These breeds are good for people who want a close relationship with their dog, or who like a dog that looks upon them as someone to worship. These dogs want to be your shadow – to follow you from room to room and to touch you as much as possible.

Other breeds do not need such close ties and will do better when alone for long hours at a time. These breeds have a tendency to be more standoffish. That doesn't mean they won't love you and want to be with you. It just means they won't be quite so demanding about it. (See the box on the opposite page).

> ### Trivia...
> Within a wolf pack, the subordinate members show affection to the more dominant members. In your family, a puppy will show affection to you. As she grows up, she will continue showing you affection as long as you remain the dominant figure in her eyes.

Trainability

To me, this is the most important factor in my relationship with a dog. For me to have a good relationship with a dog, I need to be able to train it. I also want the dog to be able to learn, to retain that learning, and to want to work for me. I am not comfortable with a dog that doesn't want to please me.

However, not everyone needs this type of relationship; some dog owners don't want to spend a lot of time training a dog. Before you choose a breed, decide what your goals are for the dog and if training plays a big part in your expectations. If it does, don't choose a breed that doesn't train well. If it doesn't, you may not want a breed that will always be looking for a job to do.

Breeds that are more resistant to training are not stupid. They are simply more interested in pleasing themselves than you. They are capable of learning very well; you just need to figure out how to teach and motivate these dogs.

■ **Poodles** *are very easy dogs to train. It is small wonder that they were once circus dogs – following obedience commands and tricks such as standing on hind feet come really easy to them.*

MORE CANINE COMPARISONS

Do you want a puppy because you find them irresistible and want one to cuddle?
Or would you rather have one who will grow up to win prizes with her tricks?

Breeds that like to be close

Australian Shepherd
Bichon Frise
Cocker Spaniel
German Shepherd
Golden Retriever
Maltese
Toy, Miniature, and Standard Poodle
Shetland Sheepdog
Shih Tzu

Breeds that are standoffish

Afghan Hound
Akita
Basset Hound
Bloodhound
Bulldog
Chow Chow
Rottweiler
St. Bernard
Siberian Husky

Breeds that train more easily

Akita
Australian Shepherd
Border Collie
Doberman Pinscher
German Shepherd
Golden Retriever
Rottweiler
Shetland Sheepdog
Standard Poodle
Welsh Corgi

Breeds that train less easily

Basset Hound
Beagle
Bulldog
Chow Chow
Dachshund
Dalmatian
Lhasa Apso
Pekingese
Pug
Yorkshire Terrier

Protectiveness

Many people get a dog for protection. Perhaps a neighbor's home was burglarized, or one of the family members travels a lot and the people remaining at home would like some additional security. In any case, many breeds were designed to be protective.

Remember, there is often a fine line between protectiveness and aggression in a dog.

If you would like a dog for protection, make sure you are also willing to do the training needed to keep the dog under control, so that its protectiveness doesn't turn into dangerous aggression.

Good watchdogs

Some breeds are recognised as good watchdogs but are not necessarily aggressive. These include: Airedales, Miniature Schnauzers, Scottish Terriers, Standard Poodles, Welsh Corgis, and West Highland White Terriers.

Protectors

Other breeds will back up their bark with actual protection for you. Some of these are: Akitas, Australian Shepherds, Boxers, Doberman Pinschers, German Shepherds, Great Danes, and Rottweilers.

Bad watchdogs

However, some breeds are not only uninterested in being watchdogs, they may even lead the burglar to your best silver! This category includes: Alaskan Malamutes, Basset Hounds, Bloodhounds (shown here), Labrador Retrievers, Brittanies, Bulldogs, Golden Retrievers, Newfoundlands, and Siberian Huskies.

■ **Bloodhounds** *are very friendly dogs, whose reputation for being ferocious is in fact undeserved. Although they are relentless while tracking, having found their quarry they will probably try to make friends!*

The idea of breeds

THERE ARE MORE THAN 400 dog breeds worldwide. How did these come about? As dogs became domesticated, people found that dogs could help them in all kinds of tasks. Perhaps one hunter found that his male dog had great scenting abilities and could follow the trail of game with ease. When a neighboring hunter had a female dog with the same skills, they arranged for these two to breed. The resulting puppies could also follow a game trail well. By breeding together dogs that shared the same skills, abilities were shaped into different breeds.

What about mixed-breeds?

A friend of mine keeps only mixed-breed dogs and thinks purebred dogs are hyper, neurotic, and mixed up. She's wrong, but many people believe such myths.

A purebred dog is a known entity; you know what the breed was designed to do (such as herding or hunting), and certain behaviors can be predicted because of this.

With a purebred dog you will also have a good idea about the dog's adult size, height, weight, and coat type. A mixed-breed dog, especially one that is a mixture of several different breeds, is very much an unknown. It may be big or small, and may be friendly or incredibly protective. A mixed-breed dog is a surprise!

A simple summary

✔ Before you choose a breed, decide which canine characteristics are important to you.

✔ Choose a breed that you will be comfortable with for coat care, exercise requirements, trainability, and ability to be a companion.

✔ There are over 400 breeds known worldwide. Each has different characteristics.

✔ Mixed-breed dogs are wonderful pets. However, since you know the genetic heritage of a purebred dog there's less chance of getting an unpleasant surprise.

Chapter 3

In the Beginning: A Puppy

RECENTLY, MY HUSBAND and I wanted a new puppy. We wanted a female, around 10 weeks of age, trainable, intelligent, but not hyperactive. So we were researching breeders and asking questions. A friend of ours didn't understand this. "A pup is just a pup!" she said. "Go and get one." Yes, a pup is just a pup, just like a horse is just a horse, but there are big differences between a Thoroughbred and a wild Arabian horse. Many factors come together to make each puppy a unique individual.

In this chapter:

✓ What do the parents contribute?

✓ Early puppy development

✓ Mom as first teacher

✓ Puppy testing

✓ Listen to your heart

EACH PUPPY IS ADORABLE – AND EACH IS UNIQUE

What do parents contribute?

A PUREBRED PUPPY has many genes in common with his ancestors. These genes control his size, type of coat, shape of tail, and much more. A puppy's breed heritage also affects his behavior. As I mentioned in Chapter 2, many breeds have characteristics that make them unique. A pup inherits these characteristics from his parents, grandparents, and more distant ancestors.

Parents contribute so many characteristics to a puppy that it is always a good idea to see a puppy's mother, and if possible his father, before you decide to take him.

Conformation

All of the physical things that make a particular breed unique contribute to that breed's conformation. These include not just physical features but also details of how these features are put together, such as the set of the ears, the tail set, the angles of his joints, and so on. These attributes are hereditary and are passed to the puppy from his parents.

Health

The parents' health affects puppies in a couple of different ways. Genes passed on to the puppies from their parents could cause health problems, physical deformities or weaknesses, or could make the puppy susceptible to problems or diseases. Certain breeds are known to have a problem with certain health threats, and although the threat itself may or may not be hereditary, the propensity to have this problem certainly is.

Temperament

Most experts believe 80 to 90 percent of a pup's personality comes from his own unique being, his environment, and training, while 10 to 20 percent is inherited. This is a significant portion. If you see a pup's mother and father, not only will you see what they look like and how healthy they are, but you'll also see what their personalities and temperaments are like.

■ **A mother dog's personality** affects her puppies. If she is fearful, shy, anxious, or overly aggressive, her puppies will feel those emotions and learn them, even when they're very young.

Early puppy development

A WELL-FED, HAPPY PUPPY will eat and sleep for most of the first 2 weeks. If a puppy seems to be unhappy, something is wrong. Perhaps the mother doesn't have enough milk or the puppy is not able to nurse enough. A variety of things could go wrong, which is why close communication with a veterinarian who has a good working knowledge of breeding and puppy raising is vitally important. A responsible breeder will watch the mom and puppies closely, assist the mother when she needs help, and call the veterinarian at the first sign of a problem.

■ **A good breeder** *gently handles his puppies every day, right from the start.*

You can get your puppy from a breeder, a pet shelter, or a pet store but a breeder is your best bet. A good breeder can show you the health and vaccination records for a puppy and his mother, tell you about any hereditary defects, and show you the mother of the puppy. You know you've got a puppy that has been kept clean, taken good care of, and that has become accustomed to human handling. (See Dogs in Cyberspace, at the end of the book, for web sites that list breeders).

Day 1 through day 14

About 90 percent of a newborn puppy's time is spent sleeping. In the first week, the eyes and ears are not open yet. The most active senses are those of smell and touch, and he uses these to find his mom and her nipples. He is able to move by a swimming type crawl, usually without lifting his tummy off the ground. As the legs get stronger from day to day, he will be crawling more than swimming.

Mom's many jobs

At this point in life the puppy cannot defecate or urinate on his own, and the mother will stimulate him to do so by licking his tummy and genitals. It is important that mom remain calm and relaxed as much as possible during this period, or her anxious behavior can imprint onto her puppies and they, too, will be nervous, anxious dogs.

Day 15 through day 21

The puppies are more awake now and do not need quite as much sleep as they did the past 2 weeks. They are still nursing quite strongly and should not yet be weaned. Some formula can be offered toward the end of this period, to introduce the puppies to the idea of food.

Let there be senses

Their eyes are opening now, although their eyesight is still quite dim. Light and dark can be perceived, as well as movement. The ears also open early in this period, although they do not focus well on sounds yet. The puppies will startle at unexpected sharp sounds at about 21 days.

Motor and social skills

The puppies are developing better motor skills now, and can crawl. Their muscles are also getting stronger through additional movement, as well as through activated sleep. The puppies' tails start to wag between 18 and 21 days. Toward the end of this period the puppies will also start urinating and defecating without their mother's help. During this period, early social skills are being established. The puppies begin to recognize their littermates and their mother. They begin interacting with one another too, chewing and pawing each other.

Trivia...

During the first few weeks of life, puppies often twitch during sleep as if they are dreaming. This is called activated sleep, and serves to strengthen their muscles. When a puppy is developed enough to stand up and walk, the exercise gained during activated sleep should make him strong enough to do so.

STAGES OF PUPPY DEVELOPMENT

Puppies are born blind and deaf. Their legs are very weak and they can just about raise their heads. But they gain physical dexterity very fast.

1 **Day 1–14**

The puppy only eats, sleeps, and grows.

2 **Day 15–21**

The puppy becomes aware of his senses.

3 **Day 22–35**

The puppy discovers the world near him.

Day 22 through day 35

This is a period of big changes. The puppies are sleeping less and are more active. Their senses are developing rapidly, with vision and hearing becoming more clear. Each puppy is also much more aware of his environment. As the puppy learns to move his head, he can better use his senses of vision, hearing, and smell.

Doing for themselves

Puppies can be introduced to soft foods now. Most mother dogs will start weaning their puppies toward the end of this period, especially because the first teeth begin to appear now. The mother dog may regurgitate semi-digested foods for her puppies, and the breeder should allow her to do so.

Physically, the puppies are stronger and are no longer crawling. They can walk, run, stand, and will even start to jump and pounce. Their vocal cords are also mature, and they can now bark.

By day 35, puppies start to leave their nest to eliminate, and if it's possible, their mom should be allowed to start taking them outside. In this way, the puppies will learn housetraining skills very quickly.

4 **Day 36–49**

The puppy starts exhibiting emotions and becomes curious.

5 **Week 8–12**

The puppy learns social rules from his littermates and mother.

Social play

Social skills continue to develop. Play becomes more important, and the puppies will play vigorously with one another. As they bite, chew, and wrestle, they become aware of their own strengths and learn how soft or hard to bite by the reactions of their littermates.

The puppies also start showing instinctive canine hunting behaviors around this time. A puppy will grab a toy, or a piece of newspaper (or a littermate) and shake his head as if to tear off a piece of meat or to break the neck of his prey. The instinct to chase kicks in now, too. A toy pulled slowly across the floor is enough to entice the puppy to chase, pounce, and grab it.

The mother dog will interfere with the puppies' playtime if things get too rough. She will also correct a puppy that shows disrespect or bites too hard. This initial discipline helps teach the puppies to accept other discipline later in life.

■ **Chewing is an expression** *of basic canine hunting instincts. At around 5–6 weeks, as their teeth develop, puppies start experimenting with this activity.*

Avoid choosing an orphan puppy. These puppies do not receive early canine socialization and can grow up not understanding discipline and not realizing that they are dogs – leading to a host of behavior problems.

Watch the stress

The breeder should start handling the puppies a little bit more during this period, but they should not be handled by many other people, as it may stress them. But the breeder and his family can massage and cuddle the puppies to accustom them to human handling.

Day 36 through day 49

The puppy begins to respond to his environment in emotional ways now. He may whine or cry when he's afraid, cry when he's hurt, and show excitement when he's playing. He is also beginning to remember things and is capable of learning.

The big explorer

At this point a puppy becomes very interested in his environment and will try to explore. He will try new things, such as investigating toys. Because of this, having a variety of puppy toys is very important now. Other things – including some very simple objects – can enrich his environment. A large, round, empty oatmeal container smells interesting and rolls very nicely. An empty plastic milk jug with a few small stones in it makes a nice sound. A cardboard box is a fun den. It doesn't take much to get puppies interested, and it is a very important stage in their development.

Many adult behavior problems (or personality flaws) have roots in young puppyhood. Adult dogs that have difficulty coping with anything out of the ordinary, including unfamiliar objects, may not have had the opportunity to explore new things as a puppy. That oatmeal box, cardboard box, or milk jug can all teach puppies to investigate new things and to be brave, instead of afraid, when discovering the strange and unusual.

Weaning time

The puppy can be weaned now, as he has teeth and is capable of eating more solid foods. He is growing rapidly and looking a little bit more like he will as an adult. His muzzle is lengthening and his ears may start to stand up (if they are supposed to.)

The puppy's mother is acting very much like a pack leader. She will be very affectionate, patient, and will even play with the puppies. However, if a puppy is disrespectful in any way, or is too rough, or tries to steal food, momma will correct him firmly and sharply.

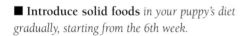

■ **Introduce solid foods** *in your puppy's diet gradually, starting from the 6th week.*

Week 8 through week 12

Most puppies go to their new homes during this period. However, special care should be taken during the 8th week of life to make sure the puppy is not frightened.

The fear period

The 8th week is commonly called a *fear period*. If a puppy is frightened at this time during, say, his first car ride to his new home, he may retain that fear of cars forever. If he is hurt during this trip to the vet's office for his vaccinations, he may always be afraid of that office. It is believed this particular period lasts only a week.

When possible, puppies should leave for their new home when they are 9 weeks old, to avoid the critical fear period.

> **DEFINITION**
>
> *The **fear period** is a crucial period in a puppy's development, during which the pup is particularly sensitive to scary objects and situations. Anything that scares him now could turn into a lifelong fear.*

Lessons begin

The brain is fully mature at this age and the puppy is very capable of learning. He may have a short attention span, but he can learn and remember what he's learned. Gentle, positive training should be started now, to take advantage of this. He can also start learning some household rules, including housetraining.

Social activities with people are very important. This is when the puppy is capable of bonding with people in general and his new owner in particular. Time must be spent caring for the puppy, teaching him to accept grooming and, of course, feeding him. It is important that he learns where his food comes from. He will also be very eager to play, and he needs to learn how to play with people. He needs to learn that he cannot bite and chew on people as he did with his littermates.

While some breeds are more prone to using their teeth than others, puppies do nip. A puppy should be told, "Acckk! No bite!" each and every time teeth touch skin or clothes.

INTERNET

acmepet.petsmart.com/ canine/genetic/article/ primer.html

Try this site for a good overview of canine genetics and other articles about canine health and behavior.

■ **At 9 weeks of age** *your puppy will be more receptive to basic training than at a younger age. Get him used to a leash, start housetraining him, and remember to be patient and gentle.*

Mom as first teacher

THE MOTHER DOG IS CARING *and affectionate to her puppies, and this is important to their survival. However, her position as the puppies' first teacher is also critical to their survival with people.*

Playing

The mother dog teaches her pups how to play together and how to play with her. She will encourage them to play with toys, sometimes even holding a toy right in front of a puppy, dangling it there until the puppy chases it. She may hold the toy as the puppy grabs it in his jaws and struggles with it, growling and tugging. She may walk away slowly, holding on to the toy, dragging the puppy behind. The variations are endless. The mother will encourage the pups to play with her or allow them to play by themselves.

During playtime, the puppies learn to give and take. They learn to be submissive when it's necessary and how to be dominant without being a bully. If a puppy turns into a bully, the mother dog will correct him quickly. Momma dog's puppies learn many of life's lessons through play, and by helping her puppies play, she is giving them a chance to learn.

■ **Puppies should spend** *as much of their early time as possible with their mother and littermates – otherwise they are never really comfortable around other dogs.*

By playing, the puppies learn what it is to be a dog; something we know is important to them but cannot really understand.

Accepting discipline

Momma dog also teaches the puppies to accept discipline and this, too, has an important effect on her puppies' future. When a puppy makes a mistake, the mother dog will correct the puppy quickly and firmly, using just enough force to do the job. She will never, ever hold a grudge. Her correction may be a growl, body language, or she may pin the puppy to the ground. No matter what the mother dog does, the puppy understands and must accept it. She doesn't give him any choice. By teaching him to accept this discipline, the mother makes it possible for the puppy's future owners to correct him, too.

Puppy testing

PUPPY TESTING is a way of seeing how puppies react to certain things. By watching their reactions, you can decide which puppy will be better for you.

These tests are best done when the puppies are 6 to 7 weeks old. Many breeders do puppy tests, so if you are talking to a breeder about her puppies, ask if she tests them. If she does, ask if you can watch the process. If she doesn't, ask her if she'll let you perform the test. Most knowledgeable breeders will want to supervise or participate, of course, to protect their puppies, but will not object to you doing the test.

Looking at the littermates together

By 6 weeks of age, the puppies are interacting with each other – playing and mock fighting. By interacting, they are learning social rules. And by watching the puppies together while they are interacting (not while they're sleeping!), you can gain some clues to each puppy's personality.

While you're watching the puppies, don't get involved. Don't interact at all – just watch them and take notes. The more you know about them while they are acting naturally, the better.

The bold puppy

The boldest puppy – which is often the biggest, but not always – is usually the first to do anything. He is the first to the food, the first to grab a toy, and the first to climb out of the whelping box. This puppy is usually a good law enforcement dog, search and rescue dog, or herding dog because he is bold. However, this could be a bad choice for someone who lives alone and works long hours, or for a senior citizen who needs a calmer dog.

■ **In a play-fight,** *one puppy may be very tenacious, but another may give up the fight quickly.*

■ **Before testing to decide** *which puppy in the litter would suit you, check for some other things. Have the puppies been kept clean? Are they active and happy, or are they overly fearful, shy, or aggressive? Are health and vaccination records for the puppies and their mother available?*

The fearful puppy

The puppy who sits in the corner by himself and watches the world go by may seem like a calm, knowledgeable puppy, but in reality this puppy may be a little fearful. Further testing will reveal whether he simply has a calm personality that can cope with life, or he is a fearful puppy that is sitting back watching for fear of getting involved.

The one in between

The puppies in between these two extremes will bounce back and forth. In one situation one puppy will be bolder or more dominant, while in another situation one of the other puppies will take over. It's important to watch and see who is roughest during play, who accepts a correction from a littermate when he bites too hard, and who always ends up on top of the puppy pile. Watch, too, and see who has a temper and who is the crybaby.

Starting the test

Have a friend or family member with you when you go to choose your puppy. Ask them to watch carefully and take notes about each pup's responses.

Tell your friend to take as many notes as possible when you are puppy testing. Once you have tested two or three, the results will start to get mixed up and you won't remember which puppy did what!

Five simple tests

Test one puppy at a time and have him do all the exercises before you go on to the next one. Take the first puppy to a room away from his mom, littermates, and other distractions.

1 **Walking away:** Set the puppy on the ground and walk away from him, without calling him or even making eye contact. What does he do?

A) He follows you.
B) He is underfoot, climbing on your feet.
C) He crawls after you, doing a belly crawl.
D) He ignores you and goes off in the other direction.

2 **Calling:** Move away from him, then bend over and call him, clapping your hands to encourage him.

A) He comes to you with tail wagging.
B) He chases you so fast that you don't have a chance to call him.
C) He comes slowly or crawls on his belly to you.
D) He ignores you.

3 **Restraining:** Roll the puppy over on his back and place a hand on his chest, gently restraining him for 30 seconds, no longer.

A) He struggles for a few seconds but then gives in and lies quietly.
B) He struggles the entire 30 seconds.
C) He cries, tucks his tail up, and perhaps urinates.
D) He struggles for more than 15 seconds, then stares at you or looks away.

4 **Lifting:** Placing both hands under the puppy's rib cage, lift the puppy up in the air (without cradling him to you) for 30 seconds.

A) He quietly accepts it without much wiggling.
B) He struggles for up to 15 seconds.
C) He accepts it with a tucked tail, some crying, and perhaps some urinating.
D) He struggles for more than 15 seconds, and then tries to turn around toward you and nip your hands.

5 **Tossing a ball:** With the puppy close to you, toss a ball or a crumpled piece of paper away from you.

A) He dashes after it, picks it up, and brings it back to you.
B) He brings it back but doesn't let you have it.
C) He goes after it but doesn't pick it up.
D) He picks it up but then takes it away.

■ **A puppy that comes** *slowly and hesitantly to you when you call enthusiastically may grow up to be a relatively shy or fearful dog.*

Looking at the results

There are no "right" or "wrong" answers for these tests. Instead, you want to use the results to choose the right puppy for you. I have tried these tests and found them quite effective. When I was choosing my puppy, Kes, I wanted a puppy that was middle of the road when it came to dominance – an outgoing puppy that wasn't fearful, that liked to retrieve, and that would accept handling. By using these tests, I chose Kes and he has turned out to be exactly what I wanted.

✓ Mostly A

A puppy whose responses were mostly A's is a middle-of-the-pack dog in terms of dominance. This is not the most dominant puppy nor the most submissive. If this puppy also scored A in the retrieving test, he will suit most families with children or active people. This puppy will accept training, and although he may challenge your dominance as an adolescent, he will accept your leadership.

The puppy that scored A's and B's will be a little more dominant and will probably challenge you more during adolescence. If he scored A on retrieving, he will accept training. If he scored B, or D on the retrieve, training could be a challenge.

✓ Mostly B

The puppy that scored mostly B's is a more dominant personality. He would grow up to be a good working dog, or a good dog for someone who is also a strong personality – particularly someone who wants to do a lot of things with the dog. A dog like this is not good for someone with a soft personality or someone who doesn't enjoy dog training, because this dog will need the structure of regular training.

■ **It's easy to fall in love** *with several puppies in a litter, but don't bring home more than one littermate. The sibling bond is strong, and those puppies will live for each other – not for you.*

✓ Mostly C

The puppy that scored primarily C's is a more fearful or reserved personality. He must be handled carefully. If the dog had B's and C's, he could potentially become a fear biter and will need positive training, a calmer environment, and careful handling that does not emphasize his fears. He would do well with a single adult or in a quiet adult home. Not the dog for an active, rowdy home environment, he is not the best mix with children.

The puppy that scored C's and D's will usually have trouble bonding with people, and when he does bond, he could become a one-person dog. A slightly fearful, cautious yet independent personality such as this is a challenge that should only be taken on by someone who doesn't want a clinging dog, and is willing to be quiet and patient. This dog will need calm, positive training.

✓ Mostly D

The puppy that scored mostly D's is an independent soul that isn't convinced he needs people. He will need to spend lots of time with his person so that he can bond. He will also need training, probably using a combination technique with lots of positive reinforcement and calm, non-threatening corrections. (These dogs usually do need corrections in their training; the positives are not enough to convince them to change their ways.) This type of personality is usually better with a family who is gone for hours each day, and rarely suffers from separation anxiety (as do the puppies who score mostly A's or B's).

Listen to your heart

CHOOSING THE RIGHT PUPPY *can be hard. An emotional decision is rarely the right one, yet the decision cannot be made totally without emotion either. These tests are simply a tool to help you choose the best puppy for you. However, to choose the right puppy, you also need to be honest about yourself.*

Use the information in this chapter and in Chapter 2, but listen to your heart as well. A puppy that performed just right for you in all the puppy tests still isn't right for you if there isn't a good feeling, too. After all, the puppy could be all A's (if A's are right for you), but could still be the wrong puppy if you don't like each other!

■ **Whichever puppy you choose,** *your relationship will be based on bonding and love.*

A simple summary

✔ Because of the genes passed to him from his parents, each pup is a unique individual, different even from his brothers and sisters.

✔ The parents' genes affect many aspects of the new puppy, including his breed heritage, conformation, physical health, and temperament.

✔ Puppies are born helpless, but their physical, emotional, and intellectual development occurs very rapidly.

✔ Puppy testing can give you more information about the puppies' personalities, temperaments, and pack orientation.

PART TWO

Chapter 4

Before You Bring Your Puppy Home

BRINGING HOME A PUPPY is so exciting! Are you, your house, and your yard ready for her? What should you have on hand? Do you know what vet you'd like to use to care for her? Do you know where you will take her for training or grooming? Read this chapter and make sure you are really ready.

In this chapter:

✓ Let's go shopping!

✓ Is your house safe for your puppy?

✓ Is your yard safe for your puppy?

✓ Finding pet professionals to help you

✓ What else do you need?

53

Let's go shopping!

YOUR PUPPY WILL NEED *some basic supplies. If you already have a dog, you may have some of these things on hand. However, if this is your first puppy, a shopping trip is definitely in order. Where you go shopping is up to you. The larger pet supply stores will have everything you need, but their prices may be a little higher than a big discount department store. Still, the discount store won't have everything you need. If you don't mind shopping around, you can compare prices at both.*

Puppy food

Find out from the breeder or shelter you've got your puppy from, what the puppy has been eating. A sudden change in her food can cause gastrointestinal upset, including diarrhea, so you will initially want to keep the puppy on her normal diet. Make sure you have a 2- to 3-week supply of food on hand the day you bring your puppy home.

If you would prefer to feed your puppy food that is different from what she had at her breeder's, change the diet very gradually over a 2- to 3-week period so that she can get used to it.

Food and water bowls

It may seem odd to list these, since everybody knows their dog will need bowls. However, bowls from the cupboard won't work well. Why? Because puppies play with their bowls, dump them over, and use them as toys. Plastic bowls will be chewed, and breakable bowls will be broken.

A metal food bowl is a good idea, and the water bowl should be unspillable. An unspillable bowl will be just as wide on the bottom as it is on top, and the bottom will be heavy.

METAL BOWL

CERAMIC BOWL

Collar and leash

Get a nice, soft *buckle collar* for the puppy. A nylon collar that you can make larger as the puppy grows is great. A 4- to 6-foot leash is fine. You may need some other collars and leashes during training, but we'll talk about those later.

LEASH

Identification

You will want to put some identification on your puppy right away. A collar tag is good to start, and temporary ones are available at most pet supply stores. Later, a permanent engraved tag can be ordered. When it arrives, put it on the collar and toss the temporary one. You can also go for permanent means of identifying your puppy, using a *microchip* or a *tattoo*.

COLLAR WITH TAG

Crate

A kennel crate is a wonderful puppy training tool. In Chapter 5 you will learn how to introduce your puppy to the crate, and in Chapter 7 you will learn how to use it for housetraining. For now, just remember that the crate you buy should be big enough for the puppy to stand up, turn around, and stretch out in when she's full grown.

When you go to buy the crate, you will find there are two types: plastic ones that are solid with barred windows, and heavy metal wire crates that look more like cages. I prefer the plastic crates because my dogs seem to be more comfortable and secure in them. However, the wire crates are sturdy and provide more ventilation in hot climates. Look at both types of crates, and choose the one you think will suit you and your puppy best. Some types of crates can also double as travel carriers for your dog.

Baby gates

Baby gates were made to keep human babies safe; put across the head or foot of the stairs, they keep a baby away from danger. Baby gates are wonderful training tools for a puppy. Use them to restrict her access to other rooms where she might get into trouble.

■ **A metal wire crate** *with a water bowl, toys, and a bed can become your puppy's personal space.*

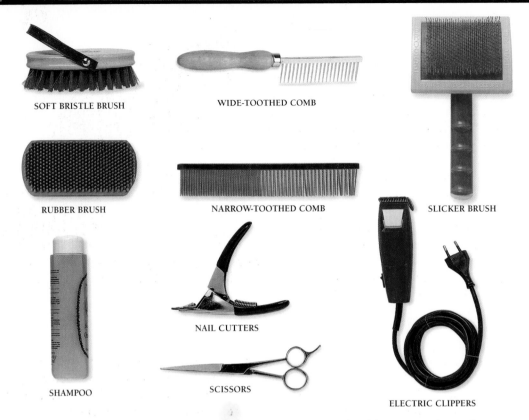

SOFT BRISTLE BRUSH

WIDE-TOOTHED COMB

RUBBER BRUSH

NARROW-TOOTHED COMB

SLICKER BRUSH

NAIL CUTTERS

SHAMPOO

SCISSORS

ELECTRIC CLIPPERS

■ **There are so many grooming supplies** *to choose from, it can be bewildering. A professional groomer can help you decide which ones to buy for your puppy depending on her breed, especially her coat type.*

Grooming supplies

Your puppy's breeder or the shelter personnel should be able to show you what grooming supplies you will need. You may need a comb, a slicker brush, or a soft bristle brush. You will also need a doggy shampoo and maybe even a dematting conditioner.

Cleaning supplies

You will need household cleaners for the dirt the puppy tracks in and for other puppy disasters. Read the labels to make sure all cleaners are safe because many are poisonous to people and animals. Never use a poisonous cleaner on something the puppy might chew; preferably don't use one in the house at all.

When housetraining a puppy, I always keep a gallon of white vinegar on hand. If the puppy has a housetraining accident, after cleaning the spot I generously dab on some vinegar. That keeps the puppy from coming back to that spot.

Pooper scooper

A pooper scooper is, as the name suggests, something to help you clean up after your puppy. A pooper scooper is usually a two-tool combination: a flat shovel and a rake or a scraper. Using this is much easier than a garden shovel. Look at the various types available at the pet supply store and choose one you think will be easy and comfortable for you to use.

Of course, you can always just pick up after your pup with plastic bags or sheets of newspaper. But a good pooper scooper will make a nasty job much easier.

■ **Use a pooper scooper** *in public places as well as at home. It makes life a lot easier and ensures good community relations.*

Toys

Looking at the selection of dog toys available in a pet supply store can be very exciting, as well as very confusing. There are so many toys! One of my dogs' favorites is a Kong (see p.239). A Kong is made of hard rubber, looks like three balls smashed together, and is hollow. The inside of it can be filled with treats or peanut butter to occupy a puppy. When thrown, it bounces weirdly, adding excitement to the toy.

Too many toys is NOT better. If your puppy has too many toys, she will think everything is hers and can be destroyed. Give her just a few toys and teach her that those are hers.

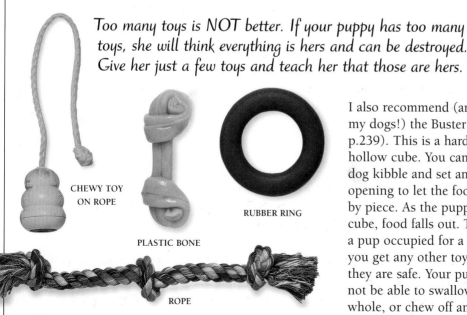

CHEWY TOY ON ROPE

PLASTIC BONE

RUBBER RING

ROPE

I also recommend (and so do my dogs!) the Buster Cube (see p.239). This is a hard plastic hollow cube. You can fill it with dog kibble and set an adjustable opening to let the food out piece by piece. As the puppy bounces the cube, food falls out. This will keep a pup occupied for a long time. If you get any other toys, make sure they are safe. Your puppy should not be able to swallow the toy whole, or chew off and swallow any pieces.

■ **Shown above** *are some common toys for puppies.*

Is your house safe for your puppy?

BEFORE BRINGING YOUR PUPPY home, you will want to make sure *your house is safe. The easiest way to do this is to get down on your hands and knees and look at your house from a puppy's point of view. You may want to do this when no one else is home because you'll feel silly, but it works.*

Pups love to chew

Puppies (just like human babies) will put everything in their mouths, so they must be protected from danger. If your puppy does eat something potentially dangerous, call (900) 680-0000 for a 24- hour poison control hot line.

Look at the lamp wire (below) dangling off the end of the table – it's inviting a puppy to chew it. Tuck it away. Tuck away all electrical cords, too. Are there magazines on the coffee table? Those will be torn up unless they are put away. How about the slippers under the couch or the knick-knacks on the bottom shelf of the bookcase? Put away everything that looks inviting and everything that is of value to you. Pick up anything that is dangerous to the puppy.

Get everyone involved

■ **Electric cords,** *telephone cords, ropes attached to curtains – your puppy can chew and tug at all of them.*

Make sure everyone in the family knows about the clean-up program, too. She needs to learn what to chew on and what not to chew on, and eventually she will, but it takes time and training. Meanwhile, prevention is the key. Put everything away!

If someone leaves something within your puppy's reach and it is destroyed, it is not the puppy's fault!

DANGEROUS SUBSTANCES IN THE HOUSE

Puppies can get into trouble just the way small children can. Take as much care about not leaving hazardous things within your puppy's reach as you would for your small but mobile child. Make sure cupboards containing dangerous substances (cleaners, insecticides, and so on) have latching doors. Cupboard safety latches work very well.

CLEANER   PAINT

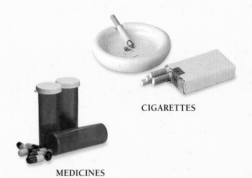

CIGARETTES

MEDICINES

a In the kitchen

Oven cleaners; cleansers; floor cleaners and waxes; bug spray; insect traps.

b In the garage

Car maintenance products, including oils, gas, and antifreeze; fertilizers; insecticides and sprays; plant care products, including systemics and fungicides; snail and slug bait; paints and paint removers.

c In the bathroom

Medicines; vitamins; bathroom cleaners; shampoos, conditioners, and hair care products; toilet bowl cleaners; makeup items, including nail polish and remover.

d In the rest of the house

Cigarettes; many houseplants, including English ivy, dumb cane, and poinsettia; many pens, including felt tip pens; laundry products.

Limit the puppy's access

Use baby gates to block off certain areas of the house and to restrict the puppy to a specific area. She doesn't need the full run of the house until she's grown up. Keep her close to you so that she doesn't get into trouble. In addition, if someone in the family isn't good about remembering to keep things off the floor, don't let the puppy into their room.

Is your yard safe for your puppy?

YOUR YARD CAN HAVE *just as many dangers as your house. Things left out can be chewed on, plants can be dug up and eaten, and inappropriate items can be used as toys. Just as in the house, try to look at your yard through the eyes of a puppy.*

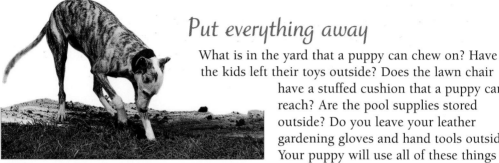

■ **You could allocate** *a digging area in the garden in which your puppy, and later the grown dog, can play.*

Put everything away

What is in the yard that a puppy can chew on? Have the kids left their toys outside? Does the lawn chair have a stuffed cushion that a puppy can reach? Are the pool supplies stored outside? Do you leave your leather gardening gloves and hand tools outside? Your puppy will use all of these things as play toys, so if you want to keep them intact, put them away.

Protect your garden

Do you have a special garden? Your puppy will enjoy it, too, so fence it off. Many dogs will help themselves to the vegetables and fruit in the garden before their owner gets a chance to pick them. Or, the puppy may think the soft ground of the garden is a good place to bury a special toy.

PUPPY TAILS: DIGGING FOR TOYS

Ebony is a black Labrador Retriever. One day Ebony watched her owner plant 100 gladiola bulbs in the garden. When her owner finished, she went inside. Later she looked out of the kitchen door and saw Ebony happily guarding a pile of bulbs. Ebony apparently thought her owner was hiding toys, and had dug up and brought to the door all the 100 bulbs!

Poisonous plants

Many common landscaping plants are poisonous, some dangerously so. If your yard contains any of the plants listed below, take precautions so that your puppy doesn't chew on them or ingest them.

- **Flowering plants and vegetables:** Amaryllis, Anemone, Azalea, Bird of paradise, Buttercup, Christmas cactus, Crocus, Cyclamen, Eggplant, Foxglove, Impatiens, Jasmine, Larkspur, Lily of the valley, Potato (foliage), Rhubarb, Snapdragon, Sweet pea, Tomato (foliage), Verbena.
- **Bulbs, tubers, and fungi:** Calla lily, Daffodil, Dieffenbachia, Hyacinth, Iris, Mushrooms, Tulip.
- **Weeds and herbs:** Belladonna, Jimson weed, Locoweed, Marijuana, Milk weed, Poison sumac, Pokeweed, Sage.
- **Trees and shrubs:** Avocado (leaves, not fruit), Bottlebrush, Boxwood, Cherry (seeds), Common privet, Croton, Dogwood, English ivy, Hemlock, Holly, Horse chestnut. Mistletoe, Morning glory, Oleander, Peach (seeds), Pennyroyal, Poinsettia, Poison ivy, Poison oak, Privet, Rhododendron, Wisteria, Yew.

Check your fence

Puppies don't realize that a fence keeps them safe. If there is something happening outside the fence, they just want to join the fun. So you must make sure the fence is secure and strong enough to prevent escapes.

Even a small hole in the fence can be chewed on and clawed at until it is big enough for a puppy to wriggle through.

Look at the bottom of the fence. Are there any gaps the puppy can dig under? Is the fence tall enough to keep the puppy in when she's bigger?

Dog run

If the fence has some weaknesses and you cannot replace the weak sections (or the entire fence), think about building your puppy a dog run. A dog run is a much better solution than chaining up a dog (which often results in problem behavior), and is safer than an inadequate fence. It doesn't have to be huge. In fact, 20 feet long by 6 feet wide is more than enough for even a large dog, as long as it has a spot that is always shady and a place where the dog can lie down off the ground. A dog run also solves many problems. It is a perfect idea if you have exotic plants or fancy landscaping in your garden that you would like to keep your puppy out of.

■ **The boards** *or wires in your fence should be tight and secure.*

Finding pet professionals to help you

A PET PROFESSIONAL *can make your life much easier. If you have a rapport with a vet, a groomer, or a trainer, you can call for advice when you have a question and have someone you trust in an emergency.*

Don't wait until there's an emergency to find that pet professional. Be sure to do it now, before you need their help.

Ask around

Most dog owners find pet professionals through referrals from other people. Ask your neighbor, friend, or co-worker where they take their dog or cat. When you see a well-behaved dog walking down the street with her owner, ask the owner where they went for training. Ask the owner of the well-groomed Bichon Frise where they go for grooming. If the same names keep popping up, that will give you a place to start.

I recently surveyed the people enrolling in my dog training classes, and more than two-thirds of them said they were there because of referrals from a former client. A few saw my Yellow Pages ads, a few saw my newspaper ad, and a few were simply driving by, but the vast majority were there because a former client said nice things about me. However, as much as I appreciate a good referral, it is also important to ask questions of any pet professional.

The right veterinarian

A veterinarian is one of the most important professionals you will find for your dog. I'll talk more about that in Chapter 9, but here let's look at how you find one. Ask each prospective candidate about your breed. Is the vet familiar with it? If you have a more common breed, such as a Labrador Retriever or a

■ **You and your puppy** *must feel comfortable with the vet. Remember, it will be an ongoing relationship.*

German Shepherd, he will be, but if you have a rare breed like an Anatolian Shepherd, he might not be. Does he know anything about the health problems of the breed? If he's not familiar with the breed, ask if you can give him some reading material so that he will be more knowledgeable.

Veterinarians have favorites, too. Some prefer to care for cats while others prefer small dogs, big dogs, or exotic pets. Ask the vet's staff if this vet has any preferences as to his clients.

Does this veterinarian have any specialties? What are they? Ask the veterinarian what his policies are regarding emergencies. Does he refer to an emergency clinic or will he take calls after hours? What are his payment policies? Does he take the credit card you prefer using? That may seem like a trivial question now, but it won't be when you get your first vet bill! Ask to see the clinic, too. Is it clean? Does it smell clean? Are the cages clean? Are the cages in an area where they can be easily supervised?

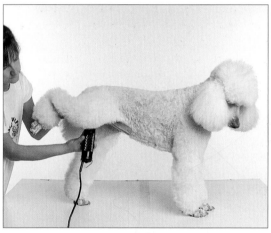

■ **Your puppy will be handled** *by her groomer time and again. Find the right one and stick to that person. Don't subject your puppy to different groomers.*

The right groomer

When you're shopping for a groomer, you can ask similar questions. Is she familiar with the grooming requirements of your breed? What products does she use? Does she use chemical flea and tick control products, or does she use natural preparations? Are you comfortable with the products she uses? How are the dogs caged while they are there? Are the cages clean? Are they easily supervised? Does she handle the animals with care and skill? What is her policy regarding payments? How far ahead must you call for an appointment?

The right trainer

You can also ask a dog trainer several questions. What type of training does she do? Some trainers are focused on competitive obedience training, which is unnecessary if you simply want a well-mannered pet. What techniques does she use? What training tools does she use? Every dog trainer has his or her own method of training, but make sure you will be comfortable with the techniques she uses.

INTERNET

www.nadoi.org

The National Association of Dog Obedience Instructors will help you find a trainer in your area.

Group training

Does the trainer you are considering offer private training or group classes? Private classes are good for a person with a very busy schedule or a dog with problem behavior, but they can be more expensive. A group class is best for a puppy that needs socialization. Ask if you can watch one of her classes so you can see what happens.

There are two professional organizations for dog trainers: The National Association of Dog Obedience Instructors and the Association of Pet Dog Trainers. Ask if the dog trainer belongs to either one.

INTERNET

www.apdt.com

This is the home page of the Association of Pet Dog Trainers. You can find a trainer in your area, or find out which books and videos their trainers recommend.

■ **Group training classes** *are a good way of introducing your puppy to other dogs, especially if you don't have other pets at home. Such training helps prevent problem behavior like aggression or fear in dogs.*

What else do you need?

HOW ABOUT A COUPLE of old towels for the puppy's bed inside the crate? Don't buy an expensive stuffed dog bed; the puppy will just chew it up. A couple of old towels will work just fine, and are easy to throw in the wash.

How about a long leash for taking the puppy out to play? If you take her to the park (after she's had her vaccinations), don't let her off leash. Instead, use a length of clothesline rope or a long leash. We'll talk about that more in upcoming training chapters, but for right now, a long leash will give the puppy more freedom to play.

That should do it. You may want to get the puppy some more toys or some rawhides for her to chew on, but you can get those later. Now you're ready to bring home your new puppy!

■ **A new puppy** *may find a warm water bottle or a ticking clock comforting, especially at night when you leave her alone.*

A simple summary

✓ You need to go shopping before you bring home your puppy. Get puppy food, bowls, leash, collar, toys, and the other necessities.

✓ Puppy-proof your house, making sure all valuables are picked up. Make sure your puppy will be protected from dangers, including electrical cords and poisonous substances.

✓ Double-check to make sure your yard is escape-proof and the fence is secure. Pick up anything in the yard you don't want the puppy to chew on, and fence off the garden.

✓ Before bringing home your puppy, find a veterinarian you can trust, as well as a groomer and a dog trainer.

Chapter 5

The First 24 Hours

EXPECT YOUR FIRST 24 HOURS with your new puppy to be the most difficult. The puppy will be missing his mom and littermates even as he explores his new home. You will be making adjustments to having him in the house. At the same time, these hours will be full of joy, as you get to know this cuddly new being.

In this chapter:

✓ When should your puppy come home?

✓ Where will your puppy live?

✓ How much should you handle him?

✓ Why is he crying?

✓ Fido, Rover, or Spot?

✓ Establishing the bond

67

SHOWER HIM WITH ATTENTION ON HIS FIRST DAY HOME

When should your puppy come home?

AS WE LEARNED IN CHAPTER 3, *the best time for a puppy to leave his mom is between 7 and 8 weeks of age. During the 8th week he will go through a fear period, and if he is frightened at the time (say, of the car ride) those fears could remain for a long time. If you can't bring the puppy home during the 7th week, wait until he's 9 weeks old to bypass that scary 8th week.*

Try for a weekend

If you work on a Monday through Friday work week, try to bring your puppy home on a Friday evening. This will give you the entire weekend to get your puppy used to his new home, his new family, and the new routine. If your work week varies, try to schedule the homecoming when you will have at least one full day at home after picking up the pup. If at all possible, don't pick up your new puppy if you will have to go and leave him alone the next day.

■ **Spending time with your puppy** *from the moment he reaches home starts the process of bonding from day one. Early bonding equals strong bonding.*

Leaving your puppy alone on the first day is a recipe for disaster. A lonely puppy will cry, scream, and try to escape. A puppy that is too lonely and afraid may fail to thrive, become sick, and may even die.

The trip home

The car ride home from the breeder (or shelter) can be very scary for a young puppy. In all probability he has never experienced such a phenomenon before! But there are a few things you can do to make his introduction to cars easier.

An empty stomach

First of all, let the breeder know when you will be stopping by so she doesn't feed the puppy for 3 or 4 hours before you come. The pup will be less apt to get carsick if his tummy is not full. You can then feed him as soon as you bring him home.

Riding in a crate

Many puppies also do better on car rides when they're in a crate. In Chapter 4, I suggested you buy a kennel crate for the puppy. This will primarily be used as the puppy's bed and to help prevent problem behavior, but crates were originally designed to keep dogs safe while traveling. What better time to protect your puppy than on his first car ride home? For the trip home, you can use a seat belt to strap the kennel crate down to keep it from moving. Your puppy can then ride home in safety.

Trivia...

What kind of music do you normally play in the car? On the way home don't play anything that is loud, rough, vibrating, or angry. This is the time for elevator music.

If your new puppy gets anxious, stick a finger in the crate and let him sniff it. A toy or two in the crate will keep him occupied. Most puppies, however, go to sleep as soon as the car starts moving.

Go straight home

Take your puppy directly to his new home. DON'T stop to pick up a few things (you bought all your supplies in advance, right?). DON'T stop at a friend's house to show him off. Leaving his mom and littermates is a big step for the puppy, and too much too soon can be frightening.

■ **Puppies feel secure** in small, enclosed places. If the crate you have at home is too unwieldy for a car, get a smaller traveling crate.

Where will your puppy live?

BEFORE BRINGING YOUR PUPPY home, you should decide where he will sleep, which areas he will be allowed in, and which will be out of bounds.

Why not in your bedroom?

I like to have my puppy sleep in the bedroom with me. Not in the bed, of course – he needs his own place. But if his crate is in the bedroom with me I can hear him when he needs to go outside. Young puppies usually need to go outside once or twice during the night for a week or two, and if you hear the puppy get restless, you can take him out before there is an accident.

I also feel that by being in the room with me, the puppy will feel less alone and more secure. Even though he is in his crate, he can still hear me snore, hear me turn over, and can smell me. He isn't alone; he is with his new family.

Into the crate

INTERNET

www.nashelter.org/
crate.html

There's information here on crate training your dog.

When you put him in his crate to go to bed (after he's relieved himself outside), offer him a treat and shut the crate door. Turn off the bedroom lights. If the puppy is restless, just leave him alone. If he cries, do not let him out of the crate. That simply teaches him that crying works (and it means he knows how to train you better than you know how to train him!). If you know that he's relieved himself and doesn't have to go outside, there is no reason to let him out. Instead, talk to him, let him know you're close by and let him get used to his crate.

Where will he eat?

Deciding where your new puppy will eat is not nearly as important as what he will eat, but it is a decision that requires some thought.

If the puppy is fed in the kitchen in the evening while dinner is being prepared, he may feel afraid he will be stepped on while he's eating. He may become nervous, which can affect his eating habits or his digestion. He may try to defend his food and show aggression when someone comes too close.

■ **A puppy eats best** *without distractions or fears about his food being threatened.*

Don't let people disturb your puppy while he's eating. He should never feel rushed or threatened. Let him eat in comfort and peace.

It is better to find a quiet spot where the puppy can eat in peace. You may want to feed him in his crate in the bedroom, in his outside run, or in the garage if he has access to a safe, puppy-proofed area there.

Where will he hang out?

When you can watch him, keep the puppy restricted to the room you're in. Don't let him wander off to another room where he can get into trash cans, chew on shoes, or have a housetraining accident. Freedom is not a right for puppies – it's something they earn as they grow up and mature.

■ **Choose an old cushion** *or mat for your puppy and place it in your living room – so you can keep a watchful eye on him.*

Limit his access

To keep the puppy close, set up baby gates to block off hallways or close the doors. Make sure other family members close doors, too, and understand the importance of restricting the puppy's access.

If the puppy is in the room with you demanding attention, but you have things to do, distract him with a chew toy. He can then still be with you but won't be annoying you.

If you can't watch the puppy, put him in his crate or put him outside in a safe place. Preventing problems is the best way to make sure your puppy doesn't get into trouble.

Where will he relieve himself?

Chapter 7 goes into much greater detail about housetraining, but you must decide right away where you want the puppy to relieve himself. Would you prefer he use a corner of the yard, or do you mind if he goes anywhere in the yard? Do you have to walk him down the street to relieve himself? Start taking your puppy to the spot you want him to use right now, in his first hours at home. If you try to change things a few weeks from now, your puppy will be very confused and you could set back his housetraining.

What you teach your puppy in the first 24 hours at home is very important.

Supervising the puppy

Your puppy will require almost constant supervision during his first 24 hours at home. No matter how carefully you puppy-proof your house, there is still a great deal of trouble he can get into if he's unsupervised. He could chew on the furniture, the carpet, or flooring. Some puppies even chew on the plaster wall board! The puppy should always be in the room with you.

Heading off danger

If your puppy never learns that the kitchen trashcan has food in it, he will be less likely to raid it. More importantly, during these supervised times, you can teach him. You can tell him to leave the trash can alone and you can give him one of his toys to chew on when he picks up your leather shoe.

If you can't watch him, he should be in his crate or in a safe place outside. He can stay in his crate for short periods of time during the day. Fifteen minutes here, half an hour there is OK, especially when he gets plenty of attention in between. If he has a safe place out in your yard, he can go back and forth between being in the house with you, to his crate, to the yard.

■ **The idea of supervising** *your puppy is to protect him from dangers as well as to protect your house from canine destruction.*

A safe backyard

Once your puppy is in the yard, always double-check to make sure the yard is safe (Chapter 4 gives detailed information about puppy-proofing a yard). Puppies can get into trouble in ways you never thought of.

To see if your yard is safe, go outside with your puppy, don't interact with him, and just watch to see what he does and where he goes.

If you're concerned about the safeness of your yard, set up a dog run. It can be temporary, maybe 6 feet wide by 12 feet long, made of fence sections securely fastened together. A tarp over part of the top can provide shade and shelter. If you set up a run like this, teach your puppy to relieve himself here.

How much should you handle him?

EVERYONE LOVES A PUPPY! *Puppies just seem to be made to hug and cuddle. However, too much handling can be very stressful, and stress is just as bad for puppies as it is for people. On the other side of the coin, you don't want to isolate the puppy. You need to find a balance, so that the puppy feels loved and welcome but is not overwhelmed by too much handling.*

Just the family

During the first 24 hours, try to limit the puppy's exposure to close family members. Invite them to sit on the floor with the puppy and let the pup come to them. If the puppy climbs up on their lap, great! They can hug, pet, and cuddle him. However, if the puppy wants to get down, they should let him move away.

People can lift the puppy to hug him or to move him from one place to another, but this should be kept to a minimum. Instead, encourage the puppy to follow you when you want him to go somewhere. Pat your leg, call him and walk slowly so he can follow. Praise him when he follows you.

■ **For a puppy,** *the family that adopts him is a substitute for the canine pack he was getting used to with his mother and littermates. He will soon learn to identify you and your family as pack leader and pack members.*

Never lift a puppy by putting your hands around his tummy. That hurts!

How to lift a puppy

It's very important to teach children the proper way to hold a puppy. They can hurt and scare him if they grab him impulsively. Place one hand behind his forelegs and the other hand under his rump, and lift slowly, gently. Make sure you support his front and back as you hold him. Holding him against your chest will make this easier.

■ **Make sure** *you hold your puppy so that both his front and the rear end are supported.*

When can your friends meet your new puppy?

After the first 24 hours, the puppy can be introduced to new people, but limit the exposure to one or two people at a time. Socialization is important, and we'll talk about that more in Chapter 8, but too much, too soon is not good. When he meets new people, ask them to kneel, crouch to his level, or sit on the floor and greet the pup calmly and softly. Again, if he wants to move away from the people he's meeting, let him walk away. At this point in his life, don't force him to meet anyone.

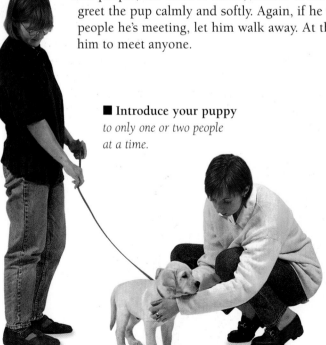

■ **Introduce your puppy** *to only one or two people at a time.*

Trivia...

Some breeds, including German Shepherds, are supposed to be reserved and aloof with strangers. Some dogs will begin showing this trait even in early puppyhood. These dogs need socialization, but should also be allowed to get to know new people gradually.

Why is he crying?

MUCH LIKE A HUMAN INFANT, *a crying puppy is usually crying for a reason. A healthy, well-fed puppy is not going to cry unless something is bothering him. Some common reasons include:*

a) **He's hungry:** If it isn't time for a meal, offer him a treat or a chew toy

b) **He's lonely:** Remember, he just left his mother and littermates. This is probably the first time he's been all alone in his short lifetime. However, he does need to learn to be alone. Keep his times alone short, letting him get used to it gradually. Distract him with a toy, a chew toy, or a ticking clock

c) **He's hurt:** Maybe he bit his tongue, stepped on a rock, or got his nose stuck somewhere. He's a baby and doesn't tolerate discomfort very well

d) **He wants attention from you:** You will very quickly become the center of his life, and he needs your attention. Give him the attention he needs, but do not let him rule your life. He still needs to learn how to be alone. Find a balance

e) **He needs to relieve himself:** He doesn't yet know how to tell you that he needs to go outside

■ **Boredom** *is a problem with dogs as well! Your house is not your puppy's natural habitat and he needs stimulation – but don't let him rule you.*

■ **Most puppies** *indicate their desire to go out by body language. They may sniff the ground or move about in circles.*

Fido, Rover, or Spot?

WHAT ARE YOU GOING TO NAME your puppy? I see more than a thousand dogs per year in my dog training classes, and am constantly fascinated by the names people give their dogs.

Get to know him first

Before you decide on the puppy's name, take a little while to get to know him. My husband and I usually have two or three names picked out. Then, when the puppy comes home, we watch him for a day or two. It doesn't hurt to call him "Puppy" for a few days. Then, as his personality appears, we decide on the right name.

Make sure, too, that the name has a good, strong vowel sound that will carry. Can you call the dog from a football field away with that name? A friend of mine named his Scottish Terrier "Magillicudy" – a cute name but impossible to use in many situations. He ended up shortening it to Cudy – an ugly name but one that was much more usable.

As you think about the puppy's name, remember this name will be his identity for 12 to 14 years. Will you be comfortable in public calling the dog with this name? Can you say the name happily? Does it suit the dog's breed, looks, and personality?

Dogs given a rough, tough, aggressive name often live up to it. I always watch dogs with names like Killer, Cujo, or Fang carefully. Think positive when naming your dog.

■ A name like "Baby" or *"Tiny" may sound exactly right now that your puppy is actually a baby. But how big will he grow up to be? Will he look like a "Baby" then?*

Teaching him his name

Once you have decided on a name, teach the puppy that this sound refers to him. Call him by offering a treat, patting your legs, and encouraging him to come to you as you say his name. Use a happy, higher-pitched tone of voice, much the way a child says "ice cream!" when the ice cream truck comes by.

■ **Call your puppy** by *his name as you attract his attention with toys and treats.*

Say your puppy's name in a high-pitched tone of voice, and when he looks at you, praise him. If he doesn't look, make another noise, like knocking on the wall with your knuckles. When he looks to see what the sound is, say his name again and praise him for paying attention.

Never use the puppy's name to scold him. His name should always be positive and happy!

A registered name

If your dog is purebred and the breeder gave you an application for registration, you will need a more formal *registered name*. Often the breeder will ask you to use his kennel name as a prefix. For example, Dax's registered name is Apache Trails Jadzia Dax. Apache Trails is her breeder's kennel name. All of his dogs have Apache Trails in their registered name.

Dax's name happens to be a part of her registered name, but that doesn't always apply. The registered name doesn't have to correspond with the dog's call name at all. My oldest Australian Shepherd, Ursa, is named for the constellation Ursa Major. However, her registered name is Little Bear of Starcross.

Registered names must be unique. If another dog already has a particular name, the registration form will be sent back to you and you'll have to come up with a different name.

DEFINITION

A dog's **registered name** *is the official name recorded with the organization where the dog is registered. Often it includes the kennel name of the breeder. A dog's call name is the name you call him every day.*

Dax
C/o Liz Palika
Tel: 555 5101

■ **It is extremely important** *to put a name tag with your address or phone number on your puppy's collar. Get him comfortable with this as soon as possible.*

Establishing the bond

■ **Forming a bond** *with your puppy is basically about investing time with him.*

THE EMOTIONAL BOND *dogs form with their owners is special and unique. Dogs bonded with their owners will do anything for them, including giving up their life. Law enforcement dogs and military dogs are often in the news because of their heroism. Just recently a police dog in my area gave his life protecting his partner. The German Shepherd Dog jumped in front of his partner, taking the six bullets a drug smuggler meant for the human police officer.*

Pet dogs are just as heroic. Cassie, an Australian Shepherd, fought a thousand-pound bull, turning it away from her owner, who was on the ground after having been gored. Many dogs have protected their owners from burglars, trespassers, and other dangers, including house fires. Why? Because they are bonded with their owners.

While the human-canine bond is eternal, it is not automatic. It must be established anew with each new puppy.

Breed and age do matter

The tendency to bond with people can vary in strength from individual to individual and from breed to breed. Some breeds bond strongly to one person or one family, while others are a little more aloof and standoffish. As a general rule, the breeds developed to work for humans, taking directions and following orders, bond more strongly than the breeds developed to work alone, following their instincts. However, there are always exceptions.

The best time for a puppy to bond with people is between 8 and 12 weeks of age. If a puppy stays with his mother in a kennel situation without much human contact until after he's 12 weeks old, he may never be able to form a strong, trusting bond with people. This type of puppy is often more like a wild animal, trusting only other dogs. However, if the puppy has good, positive contacts with people, the bond can still be formed.

It takes time

When you bring your puppy home, the bond will form as you spend time with him. Your kind, gentle, firm but fair behavior will enable the puppy to learn to trust you, to respect you, and to bond with you. You will become the most important person in the puppy's life, and at the same time, you will also be bonding with the puppy.

The key ingredient for building the bond is time with your puppy. If your puppy spends more time with your older dog, he will bond more strongly with that dog than with you. If the puppy spends long hours outside alone, without contact, the bond may never form. However, if you spend time with him before and after work, if you play with him, cuddle him, and feed him, a wonderful human-canine bond will tie you both together for life.

You'll know you've formed a bond with your puppy when you look at him and smile at him, even when he's got himself into trouble.

■ **The bond you form** *with a small puppy will last a lifetime.*

A simple summary

✔ Bring home the puppy when you will have at least 1 or 2 days to spend with him before you must go back to work.

✔ Decide right away where the puppy is to sleep, eat, relieve himself, and spend time.

✔ Supervising the puppy is time-consuming, but is necessary right now. When you can't supervise him, make sure he has a safe place to spend time alone.

✔ Handling the puppy should be limited to family members right now, and should be carefully monitored so that stress is kept to a minimum.

✔ Make sure the name you give your puppy suits him, and that you'll be comfortable using it in public for the next 14 years!

✔ The bond between owners and dogs is very special. But you have to work at it.

Chapter 6

Setting Household Rules

I T'S NEVER TOO EARLY to start teaching your puppy some household rules. By teaching her when she's young she will never learn the unacceptable behavior that often results in the dog being exiled to the backyard. Teach her as a puppy what is expected of her, and she'll grow up meeting your expectations.

In this chapter:

✓ It's your house – you can set some rules

✓ What will the rules be?

✓ Prevention is the best cure

✓ Be your puppy's leader

✓ Making yourself the leader

It's your house – you can set some rules

SINCE YOUR PUPPY IS JOINING YOU *in your house, you have every right to set some rules of acceptable behavior. After all, you're paying the bills, buying the dog food, and cleaning up the messes. You have the right to expect a certain standard of behavior.*

Right from the start

When you establish the house rules as soon as the puppy joins your family she will never learn the wrong behavior. Some owners allow their dog up on the sofa as a small pup, and when the dog is 80 pounds they want to change the rules and keep her on the floor. That's not fair! First you teach her to join you on the couch, then you get mad when she does. How confusing is that?

■ **If you want** *your dog to stay off the furniture, don't allow her on it as a puppy.*

Start teaching the puppy now, as a youngster, exactly what you expect of her. She's capable of learning – you just need to teach her.

Everyone must be consistent

Make sure everyone in the household will accept and enforce your rules. If your teenage son likes to cuddle with the puppy on the sofa and encourages her to get up whenever no one will see them, the puppy will be confused. Is she supposed to be up on the sofa or not? Everyone must be consistent with the rules.

Posting a list of the rules prominently often works. List each rule with a command you will use when enforcing it, such as "off the sofa!" This way, everyone is enforcing the same rules using the same commands. Put the list up on the refrigerator where everyone will see it every day.

Trivia...

By 8 to 10 weeks of age, a puppy's brain is fully functional and capable of incredible learning. Although she may appear to be a baby physically, she is ready and willing to learn.

What will the rules be?

WHEN TRYING TO DECIDE THE RULES you'd like to establish, think about your dog as a puppy, but also as an adult. A toy breed is easier to deal with on the furniture than a giant breed. It is also much easier to allow a small terrier in the kitchen than a tall dog that can reach the counter. Your rules should also take into account your daily routine. Of course, a dog will change your routine but you can work a compromise between your normal routine before dog and after dog. Here are a few simple suggestions for some household rules.

Is the puppy allowed in the kitchen?

Some dog owners like to keep her there because if she has a housebreaking accident, it's easy to clean up. I don't like to keep the puppy in the kitchen because there are too many dangers there for my peace of mind. I don't want her underfoot when I'm cooking or using a sharp knife. There are cleaners and other dangerous substances under the kitchen sink. Plus, when they're grown up, my dogs could easily reach the kitchen counters. So I teach my puppies to stay out of the kitchen. You can weigh the pros and cons and decide for yourself.

Is the puppy allowed on the furniture?

■ **A pup in a kitchen** *can burn or cut herself; think before letting her in.*

The owners of small dogs usually allow their puppies on the furniture; it's easier than reaching down to pet a tiny puppy on the floor. Personally, I allow my big dogs to get up on the furniture, too. Why? Because I like to cuddle with them! My dogs are not allowed to play on the furniture, but they are allowed to snuggle up on the furniture with me or my husband.

The disadvantage of allowing the dogs on the furniture is the added wear and tear, the dirt, and the dog hair. I compensate for some of that by keeping a blanket or sheet over the sofa to protect it. Before deciding whether you will allow your puppy on the furniture, think about the size your dog will grow to be, her coat, and whether you will be upset about the wear and tear on your furniture.

Is the puppy allowed on your bed?

How about the kids' beds? Many dog owners do let their dog sleep on their bed. However, this is one household rule that I feel pretty strongly about: The dog should not be allowed to sleep on your bed! She should sleep in your room, but in her crate or in her own bed. If you have a dog with a more dominant personality, sleeping with you will give her delusions of grandeur. She will think she is just as good as you are, because she also sleeps in the big bed. That attitude will make her difficult to control in other circumstances. That's why she shouldn't sleep in your bed or your kids' beds. She needs her own bed.

■ **Don't allow** *your puppy on your bed – to play or to sleep!*

If your dog is already sleeping on the bed and growls at you when you move her or ask her to get off, call a dog trainer or behaviorist for help right away. This can be a serious behavior problem that has been known to end up with the dog biting the owner.

Is the puppy allowed to beg for food?

This really isn't an acceptable habit. The puppy that begs for food usually ends up being a big pest, pawing legs, licking hands, or even stealing food. If you don't want to allow begging, make sure no one feeds the puppy as they eat, whether it's from the table or when you're snacking off the counter. No exceptions!

■ **Stealing food,** *which doesn't seem like "stealing" to a dog unless you teach her so, satisfies not just her hunger but also her hunting instincts. Keep a sharp lookout for such tendencies.*

Do you want to restrict parts of the house?

If you wish to keep the puppy out of the kids' rooms so that she won't get into their stuff, that's fine. If you have a nice formal living room, teach her to stay in the family room and restrict her from the living room. To restrict her access, close doors and use baby gates to keep her in the rooms where she is allowed.

As I have mentioned before, your puppy should not have free run of the house.

Prevention is the best cure

WHAT ELSE IS IMPORTANT TO YOU? *What will make life with a dog easier? It is always easier to teach the puppy what you want her to know, than to correct a bad habit later. By preventing problems in the first place, you teach your puppy acceptable behavior. If she learns bad behavior and thinks it's fun, changing that behavior can be very difficult. For example, if she never learns the joys of chewing a hole in the couch cushion and throwing the stuffing around you'll be able to trust her in the house alone much sooner than you will a dog that likes the fun of chewing up stuff.*

Restricting access

Part of preventing bad behavior is restricting your puppy's access. Keep her in the room with you and keep an eye on her. Don't allow her to sneak off down the hallway where she can get into trouble without you knowing about it.

You also need to teach your puppy what is acceptable and what is not. When she grabs the sofa cushion, take it away from her and hand her one of her toys instead. When she picks up your good leather shoes, take them away, put them in the closet, close the closet door, and hand the puppy one of her toys.

■ **Save the cushions!** *A stuffed object is like a toy to your pup – she'll play with it, chew it, and hunt out what's hidden inside.*

Preventing problems from happening may take some work on your part. You will have to look at your house and yard from your puppy's perspective: What is attractive to your puppy? Can she reach your potted plants? The hose is fun to chew on – can you put it out of her reach? What about the outside trash cans – are they left where she can get into them?

When she gets it right

When your dog is doing something right, give her permission to do it and praise her. For example, if she is picking up her toy instead of your shoe, tell her, "Get your toy! Good girl!" Reinforce that good behavior.

PUPPY TAILS: TRASH CANS

■ **Dogs are natural scavengers** *and most will risk trying to eat just about anything. This can be potentially dangerous.*

I made a mistake with one of my Australian Shepherds years ago. Ursa was a good puppy, so I gave her more freedom in the house. Obviously, I let her have too much freedom too soon, because she got into the kitchen trash can. Ursa was very food motivated, and she found out that the kitchen trash can had food in it. Wow! All those treasures! For years afterwards she was not trustworthy around the kitchen trash can. Even as an older dog, she would risk anything to get into that trash can, because she learned as a puppy that food was in there.

I learned something, too. My next dog, Dax, was never given the opportunity to discover the trash cans. I made sure her access was restricted and her freedom curtailed until she was old enough to be trusted. Now, at 3 years old, Dax can be trusted totally in the house. I can even leave food on the coffee table and it will still be there when I come home.

Be your puppy's leader

WHEN YOUR PUPPY WAS with her mother, mom started teaching the pups. Now it's your turn to continue her lessons. Your puppy needs a leader – an **alpha** for her pack. You, as the leader, are always fair, never asking anything that the puppy is unable to give. Praise, corrections, and commands will be given as needed, in a spirit of fairness. The leader is firm when needed, but is always affectionate and loving. The leader always demands respect.

DEFINITION

Behaviorists who study pack behavior in dogs and wolves call the top dog – the leader of the pack – the **alpha** dog.

The puppy pecking order

If you are not your puppy's leader, you will not be respected. The low dog on the totem pole has food stolen from her, gets no toys, and is often growled at, snapped at, and otherwise tormented. That should not be your position in your dog's pack!

In dog's terms, a dog that is not respected is considered weak and is low in the pecking order. The one that is not respected is dominated, often by mounting behavior.

Some dog owners want to be their dog's buddy and best friend. That is usually possible – after all, that's why we have dogs. However, it is usually possible later, after the dog is grown up and mature.

During puppyhood you must be your dog's leader, not her equal or best buddy. She must learn to respect you as well as love you.

■ **Dogs are very receptive** to body language, especially hand signals. Using body language while disciplining your puppy also reinforces you as a leader.

Making yourself the leader

HERE ARE A FEW THINGS you can do to help your puppy understand the fact that you're the leader. They are not necessarily the things her mother would do – after all, we aren't dogs. But they are things you can do that will help your puppy understand your respective places in the family pack.

(a) Eating first: Always eat first, then feed your puppy. In a wild dog pack – which we know is not the same as our family, but serves as a good example – the leaders of the pack always eat first and best. Then the subordinate pack members eat. To your dog, you should be the giver of food. This makes you very important. To maximize this importance, you should eat breakfast or dinner first, then give your puppy her meal

(b) Going through doors first: At a door or gate, give permission for your puppy to either stay behind or follow you. The puppy who dashes out through doorways is going to get into trouble. One day she may dash out the front door and end up in the street in front of a car. Or she may trip you

(c) Tummy rub: Each and every day, have your puppy lie down and roll over for a tummy rub. This is a submissive position, and even though she probably loves the tummy rub, it is still a position that teaches her to be submissive to you. This is good! As the leader, you have to be more dominant than your dog

■ **Teach your puppy** *to wait for your permission before she enters or leaves a room.*

(d) Standing over: At least once every day, as you stand up, bend over and gently hug your puppy. Don't kneel down to her level. Instead, stand over her, hugging her close as you pet her and praise her

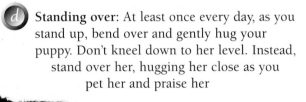

■ **Standing over your puppy** *is a dominant position and reinforces your leadership.*

e **Permitting:** Give her permission to do things. If she's picking up her ball, tell her to get her ball and then praise her for doing it. She's going to do it anyway, so take advantage of the situation

f **Enforcing rules:** Set some household rules and stick to them. As I said before, it's your house. Make sure the puppy understands that you will enforce those rules every day in every situation. No exceptions!

g **Avoid too much petting:** Don't pet your puppy every time she asks for petting. This is hard for many puppy owners, but it's important. You can actually pet your pup too much, and she will then feel that she is the center of the universe and incredibly important. Even if your puppy has become the center of your universe, she doesn't need to know it! Pet her when you want to pet her, or after you have had her do something for you, such as sitting or lying down

If you have an adult dog with a more dominant personality, do not try these exercises without consulting a dog trainer or behaviorist first.

Remember, these exercises are for puppies. An adult dog could take offense and become aggressive, especially if the dog does not view you as her leader.

INTERNET

www.dmoz.org/Recreation/
Pets/Dogs/Origins/

Try this site for a really interesting collection of articles about the history and evolution of dogs.

A simple summary

✓ It's your house, so set some rules of behavior that will make life with the puppy easier.

✓ In making the house rules, consider what your puppy will be like as an adult. Do you want a 90-pound dog in the kitchen or on the furniture?

✓ Preventing problems from happening in the first place is a huge part of teaching your puppy household rules.

✓ You must be your puppy's leader. After all, you are taking her mom's place. In fact, you want to teach her more than her mom would.

Chapter 7

The Perils and Pitfalls of Housetraining

DURING HOUSETRAINING, most owners want to teach their puppy to relieve himself outside, often in a particular area, and to be able to tell them when he needs to go outside. You should also teach your pup a command for "try to go now," so that when you take him for a walk, or when you're traveling, he'll try to relieve himself when you ask him to.

In this chapter...

✓ The importance of a crate

✓ Housetraining your puppy

✓ "I need to go!"

✓ When accidents happen

✓ The "go potty" command

✓ Practicing patience

HOUSETRAINING A PUPPY REQUIRES DOGGED PERSISTENCE!

The importance of a crate

ADDING A PUPPY TO THE HOUSEHOLD *can be a wonderful experience, but that wonder will disappear quickly if the carpets and floors are being ruined by housetraining accidents. However, there is a training tool that will enable you to train your new companion and avoid disaster. It's a crate. A crate (often called a kennel or a kennel crate), is a carrier for dogs. Originally developed for dogs being transported on airplanes, it now has a variety of training uses, including helping dogs learn housetraining skills.*

Housetraining comes naturally

All dogs are born with the instinct to keep their bed clean. When your puppy was first old enough and strong enough to toddle away from his brothers and sisters, he would do so to relieve himself. Before that, his mother stimulated him to relieve himself and she cleaned up after him. Using a crate as a training tool takes advantage of your puppy's instinct to keep his bed clean and helps develop more bladder and bowel control. It also helps him learn that there are right and wrong places to relieve himself.

Often puppies bought in a pet store are difficult to housetrain. Because they had to relieve themselves in their cage, they have lost their inhibition about soiling their bed. A crate does not work for many of them.

Close spaces between bars

PLASTIC TRAVELING CRATE

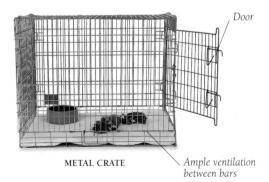

Door

Ample ventilation between bars

METAL CRATE

Types of crates

There are two types of crates available. The first type is made of plastic or fiberglass. It has a metal barred door and barred windows for ventilation on each side. The top separates from the bottom in this type of crate, so it is easily cleaned. The second type is made of heavy gauge wire, and is more like a cage. It usually has a metal tray in the bottom that can be pulled out for cleaning.

Which kind of crate to use is a personal preference. I think the plastic crates provide the puppy with more security, but the metal ones provide more ventilation. The metal ones fold up into a relatively flat, compact (but heavy) bundle, whereas the plastic ones are quite bulky. Look at the different types in the local pet supply store and choose the one that will best suit your needs.

How big?

Don't get a crate that will be big enough for a St. Bernard if you have a Shih Tzu! If the crate is too big, the puppy can relieve himself in a back corner and still have enough space to get away from it. The purpose of using the crate to housetrain your puppy is to capitalize on his instinct to keep his bed clean.

Choose a crate that is big enough for your puppy to stand up in, turn around, and stretch out.

If you want to buy a crate that's big enough for your dog as an adult, it may be too big for your puppy. Some wire mesh crates come with a divider, so you can block off part of the crate. You can also block off an area using a sturdy box such as a plastic milk crate. Just remember that your puppy must be able to stand up and turn around comfortably in whatever space is left.

Introducing the crate

Hopefully, your puppy's breeder has already introduced the puppy to a crate. However, if he didn't, or if you got your puppy from somewhere else, you will need to introduce him to the crate. Take your time doing this, because you want the puppy to be comfortable with his new living space.

■ **Don't let your puppy** *out of his crate even if he cries or barks excessively. He should learn that crying or barking will not get him out of the crate.*

"GO TO BED!" – 3 SIMPLE STEPS

1 Introducing

Open the door to the crate and toss a treat inside. Say, "Dax, go to bed!" as you urge your puppy toward the crate. Don't use your hands to urge him.

2 Familiarizing

Let the puppy go in, grab the treat, and come out. Repeat a few times until he seems comfortable with the crate. Remember, no hands!

3 Feeding

Start feeding the puppy in his crate, with the door wide open. Once he starts going into the crate with no signs of stress, close the door behind him.

Night

Put the crate in your bedroom at night so the puppy can hear you, smell you, and be close to you all night. This is 8 hours of closeness that you couldn't find the time for any other way. With the puppy close to you, you can hear him if he gets restless and needs to go outside. If he doesn't have to go outside and is just restless, you can reach over, tap the crate and tell him, "No! Quiet!"

Day

During the day, put the puppy in his crate for a few minutes here and there, whenever you are too busy to supervise him. As few as 20 minutes here or 30 there are okay, as long as he gets plenty of attention, exercise, and time with you in between his times in the crate.

Don't leave your puppy in his crate for long periods; it should not be a place of punishment.

There's no place like home!

Once the puppy is comfortable with his crate, it becomes a place of security. You can then take the crate with you in the car, strapped down with seat belts, so that he is safe. Take the crate when you travel and he will always have his own bed no matter where you go. And you'll know he is protected from danger and out of trouble.

Housetraining your puppy

NEITHER HOUSETRAINING *nor housebreaking seem to be the right words for what we're talking about. We want to teach the puppy to relieve himself outside – not in the house – and to try to go when we tell him to.*

It's simple!

With all the conflicting advice and misinformation about housetraining that bombards new puppy owners, it's amazing that most dogs do eventually become well housetrained. However, housetraining doesn't have to be mysterious or confusing. If you understand your puppy's need to keep his bed clean, limit your puppy's freedom, teach him what you want and where you want it, and set a reasonable schedule, your puppy will cooperate.

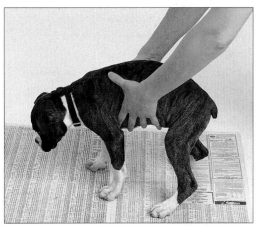

■ **It's tempting to use newspapers** *for housetraining but you should avoid doing this.*

Good teaching!

Housetraining is one of the most important skills you will ever teach your dog. Many dogs end up at animal control shelters simply because they haven't been well housetrained. Take the time now to properly teach your dog. This is too important to take lightly.

Don't teach your puppy to relieve himself on newspaper on the floor unless you actually want him to go potty in the house, on newspaper. Instead, start taking him outside right away.

Plastic scooper

■ **Always carry a plastic bag** *to pick up after your puppy in public. Invert the bag over your hand, use a pooper scooper to scoop up the feces, and then fold the bag over it. Dispose of it in the trash can.*

The first step

Take your puppy outside where you want him to relieve himself. Stand outside but don't interact with him. When the puppy starts to sniff and circle, just watch. After he has started to relieve himself, tell him softly, "Go potty. Good boy to go potty." (You can use whatever vocabulary you wish, as long as you say the same thing every time.) When he has completed his business, praise him even more.

You must go out with him to this particular spot every time he needs to relieve himself, for several weeks. Yes, weeks! You cannot simply send the puppy outside. If you do, how will you know he has done what he needs to do? How can you teach him the command if you aren't there? And how can you praise him for doing what needs to be done if you aren't there?

■ **Stay with your puppy** *while he relieves himself, reinforcing your housetraining command and praising him for good behavior.*

Establishing a schedule

All babies need a schedule, and puppies are no exception. Housetraining is much easier if the puppy eats, sleeps, and goes outside on a fairly regular schedule. Variations are allowed, of course, but not too many.

I'm not going to give you a schedule here, although many books do. That's because each puppy is different, and will need a different schedule. Start by keeping in mind that a very young puppy will need to eat two or three times a day, and will need to go outside to relieve himself after each meal. Watch your pup and you will soon learn exactly how long after eating he needs to relieve himself. He will also need to go outside after playing, when waking up from a nap, and about every two hours in between.

Let him develop at his own pace

As he gets older and develops more bladder and bowel control, he will be able to wait longer between trips outside, but this is a gradual process. Many puppies can be considered housetrained and reliable by 5 to 6 months of age, as long as they are not required to hold it too long. However, it is not unusual for some puppies to need a strict schedule and many trips outside until 7, 8, and even 9 months of age. Just as children potty train at different ages and rates, so do young puppies. It has nothing to do with stubbornness and everything to do with physical control. A puppy will be housetrained when he is ready and able to be.

"I need to go!"

IN THE EARLY STAGES OF HOUSETRAINING, you will be taking the puppy outside on schedule and teaching him the command "Go potty" (more on that in a moment). However, as he learns the command, you can start teaching him to notify you when he needs to go outside.

I don't teach my dogs to bark to go outside because, as a dog trainer I find, the most common problem behavior dogs seem to have is barking. I don't want to teach any dog to bark even more.

Just ask

I start by asking my dogs as we head towards the door, "Do you have to go potty?" I use a high-pitched tone of voice – my happy voice. This usually gets the puppy excited. Then, as we go outside to the dog's potty place, I tell him in a more normal tone of voice, "Go potty." Of course, I praise him when he does.

As the dog gets more control and can remain inside longer, I check with him, "Do you have to go potty?" If he needs to go, he starts wiggling and dancing. I praise him and take him outside. If he just stares at me and doesn't move, that means he doesn't need to go outside right now, thank you!

Later, my dogs come to me and stare at me when they want my attention. When I turn to look at them, the dogs nose my hand, or get my attention in some other way (Dax brings me a toy). I'll then ask if they need to go outside. When the answer is yes, I take the dog outside.

■ **Make sure you pay attention** *to your puppy if you're training him to notify you when he needs to "go potty." You cannot ignore him and then get angry if there is a puddle on the floor later.*

97

Trivia...

Some people have trained their toy dogs to use a litter box, like a cat. It can work, but I still recommend taking your dog outside to eliminate, no matter what his size.

Take care!

Be careful with this aspect of housetraining. It takes time and maturity for a puppy to learn to let you know he has to go out, and this maturity sets in at a different age for each puppy. Don't rely totally on your puppy's reactions for many months. Some dogs don't want to go outside and leave the happenings in the house, and will not ask to go outside even when they have to relieve themselves. You still have to remember the puppy's schedule and make sure he gets outside when it's time.

WHAT ABOUT A DOGGY DOOR?

A *doggy door* can be bought or built. It can be very useful for an adult dog, especially one that is alone for many hours. However, I do not recommend it for puppies for several reasons, listed here:

DEFINITION

*A **doggy door** is a flap that is installed in one of the doors to your house. It enables the dog to go from inside the house to the outside and back again without any assistance from you.*

a Right now, in puppyhood, you need to go outside with your puppy so you can teach him exactly where you want him to relieve himself. You need to be outside with him to teach him the words for the command to relieve himself, and so you can praise him when he does. If he goes in and out of a doggy door, you aren't part of the picture at all

b In addition, if he can go in and out freely, how do you know whether he's relieved himself? If you're getting ready to go to bed and want to put him in his crate, do you know whether he's relieved himself? If you go out with him you do know, but if he goes out by himself you have no idea

c A doggy door also gives a puppy entirely too much freedom. He ends up with free access to the house, and to a puppy home alone, that is a bonanza of stuff to get into and chew up

■ **It's not good** *for a young puppy to be able to come and go without supervision.*

When accidents happen

ACCIDENTS WILL HAPPEN. *You might as well know that now. Usually it's because you didn't stick to the housetraining schedule, or weren't watching the puppy closely enough. That makes it your fault – and it's important to remember this.*

Teach the right lesson

When an accident does happen, you must handle it very carefully. It is important that the puppy learns urinating and defecation are not wrong, but that the place where he did it was wrong. If the puppy believes relieving himself is wrong, he will become sneaky about it, and you will find puddles in hidden places behind the furniture or in the back bedroom.

If you find an accident after it's happened, do not reprimand the puppy – it's too late.

Don't rub the puppy's nose in his mess. This is disgusting, and it teaches him that the urine or feces caused the problem, which is not what you want him to learn. Remember, the act of relieving himself is not wrong; it is the act of relieving himself in the house that is wrong. Make sure your message is very clear.

Successful housetraining is based on setting the puppy up for success by allowing the fewest possible accidents to happen, and then praising the puppy whenever he does the right thing. That means every single time he goes outside in the correct spot. Every time.

Trivia...

Your puppy may leak a few drops of urine when you greet him or scold him. This is called submissive urination. Keep the greeting low-key and take him outside. If you don't make a big deal out of it, he will grow out of it quickly.

Caught in the act

If you come upon the puppy as he is having an accident, use a verbal correction: "Acckk! What are doing? No!" Scoop him up and take him outside. Then clean up the mess but do not let him watch you clean it up. (In dog and wolf packs, only subordinate pack members would clean up this way.)

■ **A verbal correction,** *given as the puppy is having an accident, works best. After the accident is too late.*

The "go potty" command

IT IS IMPORTANT *for your puppy to understand the command to relieve himself. If you take the puppy (or later, the dog) to visit someone, it is very nice to be able to tell the dog to relieve himself before going inside the house. The same thing works when you're traveling. If you stop to fuel up the car, you can take the dog out and tell him to try and relieve himself. Even if his bladder isn't full, he will try on being given the command.*

■ **Your grown dog** *will give you no trouble if you always took him out to relieve himself when he was a puppy. However, don't expect reasonable bowel or bladder control from him till he is 18–20 weeks old.*

Use the command every time

INTERNET

www.wonderpuppy.net/
canwehelp/index.htm

This site, called Can We Help You Keep Your Pet?, offers links to a wide variety of pages that deal with common canine (and feline) problems, such as housetraining, barking, and destructiveness.

Begin using a command when you first start housetraining the puppy. Tell him "Go potty," and praise him when he relieves himself: "Good boy to go potty!" It is important that he learns to associate the words with the deed.

As your puppy's housetraining gets better and more reliable, use the command when you are out on walks, so he learns to go potty in different places. Some puppies learn that they should relieve themselves only in their backyard, and their owners have a difficult time teaching them that it is okay to do it elsewhere. So teach your puppy that when you give him this command, he is to try to relieve himself wherever he may be, even if he can only squeeze a drop!

If your pup has been housetraining well and then regresses, there may be a reason. Frequent urination may indicate a bladder infection, while frequent defecation or soft stools could be caused by internal parasites. Tell your veterinarian.

Practicing patience

EVERYONE WHO HAS EVER owned a dog has a method of housetraining that works better and faster, and is more reliable than anyone else's method. Ignore the advice of your well-meaning friends. All puppies need time to grow and develop bladder and bowel control. Just establish a schedule that seems to work for you and your puppy, and stick to it. If you keep changing schedules or training techniques, you and your puppy will both be confused and frustrated.

Stick to the schedule

If you follow the right schedule, your puppy will do fine. However, a lack of accidents doesn't mean you can back off on your supervision. Instead, a lack of accidents means your schedule is good! If you back off too soon, your puppy will have some accidents and you'll have to start all over again.

A schedule that works for you and your puppy, along with careful supervision and lots of patience, will pay off. Puppies do grow up, and all your efforts will be rewarded when you find that you have a well-housetrained, reliable dog.

■ **Stick to your schedule** *while housetraining your puppy and you'll soon reap the rewards.*

A simple summary

✔ A crate is a great tool for housetraining as well as for helping your puppy develop bowel and bladder control.

✔ Teach your puppy to relieve himself outside in a particular spot and the command for this.

✔ Don't rub your puppy's nose in his accidents. Instead, supervise him better. Remember that the accidents he has are not his fault, but yours.

✔ Be patient. With a little care and discipline, accidents will pass.

Chapter 8

New People, New Things

SOCIALIZING YOUR PUPPY is one of your most important responsibilities. When properly socialized, a puppy learns to deal with the world around her – the sights, sounds, and smells of the modern world, as well as all of the different people.

In this chapter...

✔ What is socialization?

✔ Why is socialization so important?

✔ At what age is socialization most important?

✔ Fear periods

✔ How to socialize your pup

✔ What NOT to do

✔ "Keep her at home!"

A PUPPY CAN BE SCARED BY THINGS THAT SEEM COMMONPLACE TO YOU

What is socialization?

SOCIALIZATION, simply defined, is the process of introducing the puppy to life among humans. When a puppy meets people of all sizes, shapes, ages, and ethnic backgrounds, she will be less apt to shy away from people who are different. For example, many dogs that grow up in a household of only adults are rarely exposed to children. As a result, they often show shyness, fear, or aggression toward children. Having never really met children, they seem to view children as creatures from another planet. Although at times we may agree with that assessment, dogs showing poor behavior towards kids are potentially dangerous. It is important, then, that puppies meet people in all their infinite varieties.

■ **Strange as it may seem,** *an unsocialized puppy can be afraid of a small child.*

The wider world

Socialization encompasses more than just exposure to people, though. It also includes introducing the puppy to other animals. She needs to learn to tolerate the animals in your family and your neighborhood, including cats, rabbits, ferrets, and any other pets.

Socialization also includes the sights, sounds, and smells of the world. A sheet flapping on the clothesline might look like a really frightening thing initially, but if you show the puppy it's nothing serious, she will learn to investigate things that look different. A jackhammer on the street, a motorcycle roaring by, and the clang of the garbage truck are all potentially scary sounds, but when introduced properly, the puppy can learn to deal with them.

The more the puppy sees, hears, and smells — without getting frightened — the better she will cope when faced with challenges as an adult.

Why is socialization so important?

IN THE WOLF PACK, *a pup is raised in her own pack and she learns to identify those wolves. She doesn't have to get along with anyone else in the wider world; the pack is both her family and her support group. However, in our world the puppy must also be able to tolerate other people, including neighbors, meter readers, the paperboy, and others.*

INTERNET

www.wolfpark.org

To learn more about wolves, visit Wolf Park. This wildlife education and research facility studies wolf behavior.

To make matters even more complicated, in the wolf pack, as the puppy begins to grow up and hunt, she learns her home range and rarely ventures out of that range. However, we routinely go for walks with our puppy, and in doing so, we walk her across other dogs' scent markings, into other dogs' territories. We take her camping, traveling, and to get-togethers – all of which are outside her home range.

You must take time to do all of the socialization that is necessary to prepare your puppy for life with humans. You cannot be too busy right now. If you don't socialize her now, you will never be able to make up for it later!

■ **German Shepherds** *were bred to be ideal guard dogs – big, loyal, and fiercely protective. But in modern, urban, community life, these instincts need to be honed.*

Working instincts

Socialization can also affect many breeds' working instincts. During our history together, humans have developed many breeds of dogs to guard our property or livestock against other people or predators. These breeds – which include many of the herding and working breeds – are, by design, more suspicious. In our busy world a dog with these instincts could not cope unless well socialized as a puppy. Because we ask so much of our dogs that is contrary to their ancient behavior and working instincts, socialization is important. It gives the dog the skills to cope with our world.

At what age is socialization most important?

BASIC SOCIAL SKILLS *begin as early as the 3rd week of life. At that age the puppy discovers her brothers and sisters and learns to recognize them. By the 4th and 5th week of life, the puppy is more aware of the world around her and interacts more and more with her mother and her littermates. The mother dog will start correcting the puppies, and this social behavior teaches the puppy that life has rules that must be followed.*

The breeder's role

The breeder should be handling each puppy individually from the 3rd week to introduce them to human interaction. During the 6th and 7th weeks, the breeder must be very involved with the puppies, spending as much time as possible with them. The pups can learn a lot about people now, and gentle handling is very important. Play time with people is also good, although the play must be gentle to help build trust in people. There should be no rough, tough, scary play.

■ **By massaging,** *cleaning, and cuddling the puppies, the breeder can teach them that human touch is safe, comfortable, and pleasurable.*

Your role

After you bring your puppy home, socialization continues to be very important. During weeks 8 through 12, she needs to meet lots of different people and other animals, and see and hear all the new (to her) things in this world. Socialization continues throughout puppyhood, but the period between 8 and 12 weeks of age is the most important.

Dogs that were isolated from people as puppies, especially during the critical 8- to 12-week age span, will never be able to form a good, strong attachment to people later. Even when they are born to dogs who were attached to people, these isolated pups will act more like wild animals than domesticated dogs.

Fear periods

DURING THE PUPPY'S *8th week of life, she will go through what is called a fear period. At this age, she has become very aware of the world around her, and may find it very scary. Puppies show they are in this fear period in many different ways. Some will become cautious about everything, approaching objects (even familiar things) tentatively. Other puppies will be more selective, acting bold about some things and cautious about others.*

Avoid the scary stuff

It is important at this age that you try to prevent frightening things from happening. During fear periods, you will need to plan your outings carefully to avoid fearful situations. Take some treats with you, too, and use them as a distraction when something happens that could be frightening.

If you do encounter something that scares your pup, do not reinforce her fear. If you do, she will remain afraid and that fear will stay with her.

For example, if she is frightened by a fire engine's siren on the car ride home, you should be matter-of-fact about it and try to distract her. If you cuddle her and soothe her with "Don't be afraid, baby," she will take it as praise for being afraid and will think being afraid was the correct response. Since you don't want her to be afraid of sirens and other loud, shrill noises, distract her with a toy or a pat and don't make a fuss.

Handling the fear

You can do several different things to handle your puppy's fear. First of all, talk to her. Use either your calmest, most businesslike voice, or use a higher pitched, fun tone of voice. You can distract your puppy by turning her away from whatever scared her. When you turn her away, offer her a toy or a treat: "Here! What's this? Here's your ball!" Make her think about something else.

■ **Don't soothe your puppy** *when she is afraid – hard as it is. You'll just be teaching her that being afraid brings positive rewards.*

If the object of her fear is accessible, walk up to it, touch it, and show her it isn't as scary as she thought. Pat it and tell your puppy, "Come see!" If she walks close to it, praise her enthusiastically. If she is really afraid, however, and plants her feet, don't force her to go up to the object of her fear. You can touch it, but let her sit back and look at it. When she's ready, let her go up to it. If you force her, you may make the fear worse.

Ongoing socialization

Most dogs are not mentally grown up until they are at least 2 years old, and socialization is a big part of that mental maturity. I am always exposing my dogs – even my adult dogs – to different things. On any given weekend, we may play at the playground, go to a different park, or watch a marching band. My dogs have swum in the ocean, visited with Alzheimer's patients, and ridden on a San Francisco cable car. And they take it all in stride.

■ **Although the most important** *socialization period is early puppyhood, socialization is an ongoing process until the puppy's second birthday. Continue exposing her to objects, events, or people she hasn't met before.*

OTHER FEAR PERIODS

Your puppy will go through other fear periods as she grows up. Some puppies have a short fear period at about 4 months of age, and others go through one at about 14 months. You might think a dog 14 months old is grown-up, but that's not true. A 14-month-old dog is an adolescent and is still mentally immature. This is usually the last fear period most dogs go through, but it should still be treated the same way you handle fear periods in puppies.

A friend's 14-month-old Newfoundland was very obvious about her fear period. She started barking at a picnic table which had been in the same spot since she was a pup, but apparently she just noticed it. My friend had to walk her up to the table and coax her to sniff it before she would stop barking at it.

How to socialize your puppy

MUCH OF YOUR PUPPY'S socialization can be as simple as allowing her to meet new people. Take her outside and introduce her to your neighbors. Let her meet the neighborhood kids, the retirees, and the teenagers. Let her meet people of all ages, sizes, shapes, and ethnic backgrounds.

Take her along

You can also plan a few outings so that your puppy can go to different places and meet other people with you. Take her to the pet supply store with you. Let her meet the sales clerks and the other customers, and then reward her by letting her pick out a new toy. In the pet supply store, your puppy can also learn how to walk on slippery floors and see things she wouldn't see at home (such as display shelves and stacks of aquariums). She can also learn to walk next to a shopping cart – something that is very different!

Go for a walk by the local elementary school while the kids are at recess. Let the puppy hear all the children laughing, screaming, and shouting. Let her watch them run and play. If you stop by after school, let one or two kids (not a whole crowd!) pet her very gently and give her a treat. Go for a walk by the local nursing or retirement home. If some of the residents are outside, introduce your puppy and ask if they would like to pet her.

Visiting the vet "socially," without an appointment, helps make the vet's office someplace special to go, instead of someplace scary.

■ **Make the vet's office** *less intimidating – take your puppy there when she doesn't have an appointment. Just walk her in, have the receptionist give her a treat, and then leave.*

■ **If you don't have other pets,** *make sure that you introduce your puppy to other animals, so that she isn't just surrounded by humans all the time.*

Meeting other animals

If one of your neighbors has a healthy, vaccinated adult dog that is good with puppies, introduce the two. Let them play, if you can.

Do not introduce your puppy to every dog in town. Socialize only with healthy, vaccinated, well-behaved dogs that are safe with puppies. Don't be afraid to ask questions to protect your puppy!

Enroll your puppy in a puppy kindergarten training class. Not only will this help you train her, but it also provides wonderful socialization to other puppies and other people.

Ask your neighbor if your puppy can meet their pet rabbit. Hold her carefully and encourage her to gently sniff the rabbit. Don't let her chase the bunny; remember, you want to teach your puppy good manners! If you can, introduce her to other pets, including cats, ferrets, birds, and tortoises.

INTERNET

www.tamebeast.com/
index.html

The Tame Beast is a huge clearing house for links to other companion animal sites. You'll find your way to everything doggie here.

NEW SOUNDS, NEW SIGHTS, NEW SMELLS

Introduce your puppy deliberately but gradually to new sights, sounds, and experiences around the house as well as outdoors, so that she loses her fear of the unfamiliar.

INDOOR SOUNDS

- A vacuum cleaner
- A dishwasher
- A garbage disposal and trash compactor
- A plastic garbage bag being shook open
- A plastic bag being popped
- A crumpled paper bag
- A broom and mop being used
- Balloons bursting
- A metal cookie sheet being dropped to the floor

■ **Children's toys,** *especially those that move or make a noise, can frighten a young puppy.*

OUTDOOR SOUNDS

- A car engine being revved
- The trash truck out front
- The lawn mower
- A weed whacker and a leaf blower

MOVEMENT

- Walking up and down stairs
- Walking over a wooden footbridge
- Walking over a metal manhole cover
- Taking an elevator
- Walking on carpet, slippery floors, and rubber matting

■ **A motorcycle** *zooming down the street can be pretty scary to an uninitiated pup.*

OTHER ANIMALS

- Cats
- Rabbits
- Ferrets
- Goats, cows, and sheep
- Horses

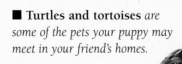

■ **Turtles and tortoises** *are some of the pets your puppy may meet in your friend's homes.*

What NOT to do

OVERWHELMING YOUR PUPPY *is just as bad as not socializing her at all. Socialize her gradually over the first few months. In her first week at home, introduce her to things around the house. If she is frightened, don't reinforce her fears. Keep things upbeat and matter-of-fact. During her second week, take her outside a little, introduce her to a few things around the neighborhood, and let her meet some new people. Each week, you can introduce her to different things. If the puppy seems overwhelmed, stop and relax for a little while.*

Control the situation

When your puppy meets new people, you must control the situation. If you think something is wrong, stop it. Remember, the whole idea is to make these outings fun and to build social skills, not to scare the puppy. When she meets new people, let her meet two or three people at a time, no more. If five or six kids swoop down on her, make several stand back and wait. They can pet her when the first group is through. Some things you must control to protect your puppy are:

1. Don't let people – kids or adults – run in the vicinity of the puppy.

2. Don't let kids scream and yell while playing with the puppy.

3. Don't let people grab your puppy and hug her

"Keep her at home!"

YOUR VET WILL *probably tell you to keep your puppy at home until she has received all her vaccinations. Until then, she may be at risk of picking up a contagious disease from unvaccinated dogs. However, I have just finished telling you to take your puppy out into the world, to introduce her to people and other animals, and to enroll her in a kindergarten puppy class. Obviously, there is a conflict here!*

The good news for a new puppy owner is that you can socialize your puppy and keep her safe too.

Keeping your pup safe

Your veterinarian is concerned about your puppy's health. As a dog trainer, I am concerned about the serious consequences of a lack of socialization. But with a few, simple precautions you can circumvent this problem. In the next chapter, I'll tell you about the vaccines your puppy will needs to be given to keep her safe, such as Distemper, Hepatitis, Parainfluenza, Parvovirus, and Leptospirosis.

Don't take your puppy anywhere near strange dogs, especially dogs that may be unvaccinated, until she has had at least two full sets of shots. However, you may let her play with a dog who, you know for a fact, has been vaccinated (your neighbor's dog for instance).

Most of the dangers to your puppy's health come from unvaccinated dogs and their wastes. You might encounter unvaccinated dogs in the park, or walking in the woods. Keep her away from them and don't let her sniff other dogs' feces and urine. Keep her away, and pull her away quickly if she tries to sniff.

■ **Most puppies have** *good immunity after their second set of shots. Many kindergarten puppy classes will not allow puppies to attend if they have not had these two sets of shots.*

A simple summary

✔ Socialization is the process of introducing your puppy to the world around her, including people of all sizes, shapes, ages, and ethnic backgrounds.

✔ The puppy also needs to see, hear, and smell different things.

✔ Socialization is an ongoing process, but is especially important between 8 and 12 weeks of age.

✔ During socialization activities, it's important to protect your puppy without reinforcing her fears.

✔ By being careful and controlling all interactions, you can socialize your puppy before she has fully finished her immunizations.

PART THREE

A SICK PUPPY CAN GET YOU DOWN

Chapter 9

The First Visit to the Vet

I KNOW YOU READ Chapter 4 and have already researched local vets before bringing home your puppy. As I mentioned there, if you have already picked out a vet, you won't need to go through the Yellow Pages in a panic once you have the puppy. The vet you choose is vital to your puppy's good health, so make sure you are comfortable with his or her professional skills, bedside (or tableside) manner, emergency procedures, location, payment policies, and staff.

In this chapter...

✓ **The first exam should be on the first day**

✓ **Vaccinations**

✓ **Potential problems with vaccines**

✓ **Make each vet visit fun**

The first exam should be on the first day

IDEALLY, THE VETERINARIAN should see your puppy within the first 24 hours after you bring him home. Why do you need to bring the puppy in so quickly? There are several very important reasons.

You need to know

There is a possibility the veterinarian could discover congenital defects you might not be able to see. If the puppy has untreatable or potentially expensive health problems, or is generally unhealthy, you have the right (if you so desire) to return the puppy to the breeder. If the puppy has a problem and you decide to keep him anyway, the breeder should be willing to give you a full or partial refund.

If you have bought your puppy from a breeder, you need to make sure the puppy is healthy.

If you adopted the puppy from a shelter or breed rescue group, you should still have the vet see him right away. If you discover potential health concerns that you might not be able or willing to deal with, you can return the puppy before you become so emotionally attached that you cannot return him. If you decide to keep the puppy, knowing about the health concern early may help you deal with it – depending upon the problem, of course.

■ **A dog shelter** *will not be able to show you a puppy's mother, or give information about breeding background or genetic disorders that may have been inherited.*

You will also want to have the vet see the puppy right away if you have another dog at home. Your new puppy can be started on a vaccination schedule, and you can make sure the puppy is healthy and not a health threat to the dog at home.

Arrange it in advance

You can actually call and make your first appointment before bringing home the new puppy. Many veterinarians' offices book several days in advance. So if you have made arrangements to bring the puppy home on Friday evening, call on the Monday or Tuesday before to make an appointment for Saturday morning. This way, you won't have to scramble to find a time to bring the puppy in, and you can be assured the vet will be able to see your puppy right away.

■ **Having your puppy** *examined by a vet should be your top priority, no matter where you got him from, or what the circumstances.*

Be prepared

When you call to make the appointment, make sure you tell the receptionist this is your new puppy's first visit. She will ask you some information about the puppy to start his health record, and she will tell you to bring in some of the puppy's stool.

The stool will be checked for signs of internal parasites. Bring in a small piece (half a teaspoon is enough) of that morning's stool. To collect a sample, invert a plastic sandwich bag over your hand, pick up the stool and then pull the plastic bag off your hand, over the stool and seal it. Don't forget to bring the sample with you!

Remember, the fresher the stool you give for your puppy's stool test, the better, because as the stool ages and dries out, signs of parasites are harder to see.

The first exam

The veterinarian's first exam will be quite thorough. He will also want to know as much as possible about your puppy's previous care. The breeder may have dewormed the puppy before you took him, or may have given the puppy his first vaccinations.

Make sure you give the vet as much information as you can, so he can help you make the right choices for your puppy's care.

BASIC EXAM CHECKS

During the first examination, the vet is trying to do a blanket check for any possible diseases or weaknesses that your puppy may have.

a Eyes

The vet will check your puppy's eyes. Ideally, a puppy's eyes should be clear, not cloudy, and should have no discharge. Unhealthy looking eyes can indicate the presence of diseases elsewhere in the body, as well as in the eyes themselves.

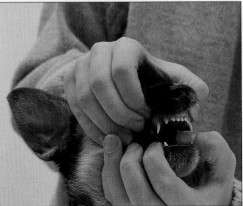

b Mouth

The vet will check your puppy's mouth. The tongue should be a healthy pink color. The gums should have no inflammation and should also be pink (not pale which suggests anemia, or yellow which indicates a liver problem). The teeth will also be checked.

Checking for internal parasites

By the time the vet finishes his exam, the stool sample will have been processed. If there are any internal parasites they can be treated with a tablet or an injection, depending upon the parasite, the vet's opinion, and the health of the puppy.

After the first exam is the time you should ask your vet any questions or express any concerns about your puppy's health.

c Ears

The ear canals should be dry, without any discharge or deposits. The vet will also check that the ears are healthy in color and no foreign matter is present.

d Glands

If your puppy's lymph nodes or glands are swollen, it indicates an infection in that part of the body.

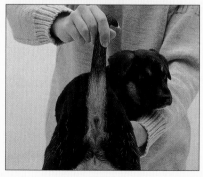

e Anal region

The vet will check the glands in your puppy's anal region and will look for indications of tapeworm. He will also check the consistency of the puppy's feces, as diarrhea could indicate a problem.

Vaccinations

WHEN YOUR PUPPY WAS BORN, *the immunities he received from his mother's milk helped protect him. But by the time he is about 12 weeks old, his own immune system must develop the ability to protect him. The immune system does this by producing antibodies – substances that protect the body from invaders. Vaccinations are based on this biological process, as explained in the box below.*

THE COMMON VACCINATIONS

When disease invades the body, the body produces a special substance called "antibody" to deal with that specific disease. So puppies (and people) develop antibodies to each bacterial or viral infection they encounter. If the puppy's body can produce these antibodies fast enough, he won't get sick.

Vaccinations work by giving the puppy a dose of an infectious agent that has been treated or killed, so the puppy can develop the right antibodies without the threat of getting sick. Most vaccinations stimulate the body to produce enough antibodies to protect it for a specific length of time. Booster shots are then given regularly for these particular diseases.

The vaccines	About the disease
Distemper	Viral infection. Affects skin, eyes, nerves
Hepatitis	Viral infection. Affects the liver. Starts in throat but spreads to other organs
Leptospirosis	Bacterial infection. Affects kidneys
Coronavirus	Viral infection. Causes severe dehydration, especially among puppies
Parvovirus	Viral infection (this virus continues to mutate). Affects intestines and bowels
Adenovirus	Viral infection. Affects respiratory system
Parainfluenza	Viral infection. Affects respiratory system
Bordetella bronchiseptica	Bacterial infection. Affects respiratory system
Lyme disease	Bacterial infection. Affects nerves and joints severely, often permanently
Rabies	Viral infection. Affects the brain

Kinds of vaccines

There are two kinds of vaccines, or rather two kinds of modified
infectious agents, given to the body during vaccination:

*A vaccine is either a modified live virus or
a killed virus. Modified live virus is more effective
at stimulating the body to produce antibodies, but
it can also cause the disease. Killed virus is
considered much safer by most experts.*

DEFINITION

*In a **modified live vaccine**, a
live organism is altered to
decrease its virulence. A
killed vaccine contains dead
organisms, but still stimulates
the body to produce antibodies.*

Symptoms	How the disease spreads	Mortality
Discharge from nose and eyes	Through dog feces or air	Fatal
Sore throat; dog doesn't want to swallow, eat, or drink	Direct contact with urine or nasal discharge	Fatal; dog can die within 2 hours of showing symptoms
Fever, vomiting, dehydration	Urine, urine-affected water	Fatal
Mild to extreme diarrhea; blood in stool in severe cases	Through dog feces	Not fatal
Vomiting, dehydration, diarrhea, specially in puppies	Through dog feces and vomit	Fatal; most dangerous canine virus. Can mutate
Coughing.	Through air by dog cough	Not fatal; but puppies at risk
Coughing; may turn into flu	Through air by dog cough	Not fatal
Coughing, and other respiratory problems	Contact, and through air by dog cough	Not fatal; but puppies can become quite sick
Fever, muscle soreness, weakness, joint pain	By infected ticks, fleas, and flies	Not fatal
Staggering, drooling, seizures, changes in behavior	Contact with infected animals (bat, skunk, squirrel, fox)	Fatal

A PUPPY VACCINATION SCHEDULE

Just as most veterinarians have their own recommendations concerning vaccines, they also set up their own vaccinations schedules for puppies. A sample schedule might look like the one in the box given below. This chart offers a schedule for initial vaccinations, but booster shots are given 1 to 3 years after these vaccinations.

Your vet may have a similar schedule or may have a totally different one, especially if he or she recommends a different combination of vaccines.

8 weeks	10 to 11 weeks	13 to 15 weeks	16 to 18 weeks
• Distemper	• Distemper	• Distemper	• Rabies
• Hepatitis	• Hepatitis	• Hepatitis	• Bordetella
• Leptospirosis	• Leptospirosis	• Leptospirosis	
• Parainfluenza	• Parainfluenza	• Parainfluenza	
• Parvo (often given as a combination shot, called DHLPP)	• Parvovirus	• Parvovirus	
	• Bordetella	• Lyme disease	
• Lyme disease			

■ **Talk to your vet,** *find out which vaccines she recommends, why, and at what age. If you would like your puppy to get a vaccine your vet doesn't recommend, ask her about it. Perhaps the disease is not found in your area, or maybe she has another reason.*

Which ones does your puppy need?

Most vets will recommend a vaccination plan for your puppy. Their recommendations will be based on their clinical experience, and on what diseases are prevalent in your part of the country. All recommend vaccines for distemper, leptospirosis, parvovirus, and hepatitis. In most parts of the country, the rabies vaccine is required by law. Some vets suggest corona and bordetella. Several years ago, only a small number of vets recommended puppies get the Lyme disease vaccine, but now many recommend it.

It's your puppy and your puppy's health, so don't be afraid to ask your vet questions about the vaccinations he or she recommends.

Potential problems with vaccines

EVEN THOUGH MODERN VACCINATIONS *have saved thousands of dogs' lives, there are still potential problems with vaccines. For example, some dogs develop a sterile abscess at the site of the injection. This is a hard lump under the skin, which will go away on its own.*

Allergic reactions

A worse problem is the allergic reaction that some dogs have to vaccines. Reactions can be as mild as a lack of energy for a day or two, or as severe as anaphylactic shock (a potentially fatal shock brought on by vulnerability to injected foreign matter). Some dogs will show other symptoms that may take a week or two to develop, and these reactions may range from lethargy or lameness, to seizures or thyroid problems.

Because of the concern about reactions, you should remain at the vet's office for at least half an hour after your puppy receives a vaccination. Severe reactions that are life-threatening, such as anaphylactic shock, will occur relatively quickly, and if you're still in the office, treatment can be started immediately.

Too much of a good thing?

Many veterinarians and dog owners are concerned that too many vaccines may overwhelm the puppy's immune system. Because of this, a different vaccination schedule may be set up, giving the vaccines over a longer period of time.

Some experts are also concerned about the numbers of vaccines being given. Modern medicine has given us vaccines to prevent many diseases that used to kill vast numbers of dogs, but in return, larger numbers of dogs are suffering from immune system disorders, and many more dogs seem to be dying of cancer at younger ages. These problems have not yet been directly linked to vaccinations, but enough people are concerned that questions are being asked.

Just because there are potential problems from vaccinations doesn't mean you should not vaccinate your puppy. Before these vaccines were available, thousands upon thousands of dogs died from diseases that are now preventable.

Less often?

Some experts are now suggesting that vaccinations be given over a longer period of time and that fewer combination vaccines be given.

Instead of giving DHLPP (distemper, hepatitis, leptospirosis, parvo, and parainfluenza) combination, the vaccine can be broken down and given as a DHL one week, parainfluenza can be given 2 weeks later, and 2 weeks after that parvo can be given.

Unfortunately, this too, can cause problems. The vaccines are normally given during the period of time when the immunity the puppy received from his mother is wearing off, and his immune system is developing its own antibodies. The puppy is in danger of catching diseases during this time, and the vaccinations can help protect him. If the vaccines are spread out over too long a period, he can get sick. And many of these diseases, especially parvo, are common and are often fatal.

Ask your vet

So on one hand you have potential dangers from the diseases themselves, and on the other hand you have the potential dangers from the vaccines. What can you do? First of all, talk to your veterinarian. Express your concern. What vaccines does he use? Are they modified live or killed vaccines? What brand does he use and how is their safety record? Is he seeing any vaccine-related problems? Is he seeing any of the common diseases in his practice, especially parvo? What does he recommend you do?

Only vaccinate a healthy puppy

Only vaccinate your puppy once he has received a clean bill of health from your vet. If he has a health problem of any kind, do not vaccinate him until it clears up. There is more of a risk of a vaccination reaction when a pup isn't healthy, because the puppy's immune system will not tolerate the shot as well.

Then, when you do vaccinate your dog, no matter what the schedule, watch him closely. Report any reactions – any at all, even sleepiness – to your vet and ask that they be recorded in your puppy's health record. A minor reaction now may give clues to related health problems later.

A vitamin B complex supplement started a few days before each vaccination and continued for a few days after will help your puppy's body cope. Give him one quarter to one half (depending upon his size) of an adult human dosage, twice a day.

■ **To ensure your puppy's good health,** *you'll need to vaccinate him, because dogs have not evolved any protection of their own against many of the relatively new diseases in canine history. Don't be worried about possible complications, such as allergies. Be informed, be prepared, and keep taking your vet's advice.*

Make each vet visit fun

BECAUSE THE VETERINARIAN *is your partner in your puppy's good health, you will want your puppy to enjoy his visits there. If he is stressed and afraid, examinations and treatments will be much more difficult. In addition, when your puppy is stressed, his body goes into overdrive with heart rate, blood pressure, respiration, and everything else increasing dramatically. It is much harder for your veterinarian to see what is normal and what is a problem when your puppy isn't relaxed.*

INTERNET

www.doglogic.com/
vaccinemain.htm

This page, written by Jean Dodds, DVM, looks at some of the controversies surrounding the traditional annual vaccination.

Offer distractions

Keep the visits fun by having staff members offer your puppy a treat when he comes in. They can also pet him, rub his tummy, and talk to him in a happy tone of voice.

When he is afraid, don't reinforce those fears. If you coddle him, talk to him softly and say, "It's OK honey, don't be afraid," he will assume your soft talk is telling him he was right to be afraid. Instead, distract him from his fears. Offer him a treat or a toy.

■ **Bring one of your puppy's toys** *to the vet's office. Let him play with it. Participate in the play, so that there can be a smooth transition from playing to examining and treatment.*

You can also rub his tummy. If he's afraid of something specific, like standing on a scale, make it fun. Stand on it yourself and let him watch you. Then encourage him to walk on it.

Stop by for a visit

Try to stop by the vet's office a few times when your pup doesn't need any care at all. Walk him in, ask the staff to make a fuss over him, offer him a treat, and then leave again before anything scary happens. Your puppy will remember those positive visits, too, and they will help him overcome any less happy visits.

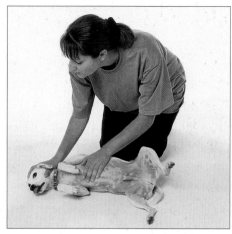

■ **All puppies** *love a tummy rub! Your touch soothes your puppy as his mom's licking did.*

When your puppy is getting his temperature taken, his ears examined or is getting a shot, you can help distract him. Hold him as close as you can, talk to him in a happy tone of voice, and with one finger, rub his head between his eyes. Most puppies will concentrate on this and forget what else is happening.

A simple summary

✔ Your veterinarian is your partner in your puppy's health care.

✔ Bring your puppy in to see the vet within his first 24 hours at home.

✔ The first exam will be very thorough, so your vet can get to know your puppy and establish exactly how healthy he is.

✔ Vaccinations are essential to save your puppy from infectious, sometimes deadly, diseases.

✔ Vaccinations can be life-savers but do not come without some risks.

✔ Make each visit to the vet's office fun, so your puppy will like going there and will not be quite as stressed.

Chapter 10

Maintaining Your Puppy's Health

M AINTAINING YOUR PUPPY'S good health is an ongoing project. Exercise and playtime are crucial. Spaying and neutering are also important for several reasons, including your pup's long-term health. And accidents can always happen. You should cooperate with your vet and learn some rudimentary first aid techniques yourself.

In this chapter...

✓ *Exercise and playtime*

✓ *Playtime should be fun*

✓ *Spaying and neutering*

✓ *Working with your vet*

✓ *Treating your pup at home*

Exercise and playtime

A HEALTHY YOUNG PUPPY *will need several exercise periods every day. She will need time to use up energy, burn calories, and strengthen her bones and muscles. This exercise will also help her learn to control her body and become more coordinated.*

The right exercise for the right pup

Exercise for a young puppy must be carefully tailored to her age, physical abilities, and breed. A 10-week old Papillon puppy is very tiny and fragile because of her build, but is more coordinated than the much larger but more rapidly growing St. Bernard puppy. The Papillon puppy will be able to move faster, balance herself better, and twist and turn better than the larger puppy.

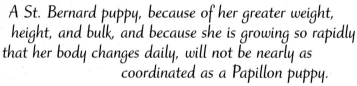

A St. Bernard puppy, because of her greater weight, height, and bulk, and because she is growing so rapidly that her body changes daily, will not be nearly as coordinated as a Papillon puppy.

Trivia...

Too little exercise, training, or owner attention, can make a puppy destructive. Some breeds that are known to have destructive tendencies, especially when young, are Siberian Huskies, German Shepherds, West Highland White Terriers, Dalmatians, Scottish Terriers, Miniature Schnauzers, and Beagles.

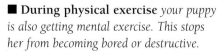

Don't tire your puppy

When exercising your puppy, make sure she can perform the exercise without getting sore or overly tired. A nap after exercise is normal, but an exhausted, extended sleep is not. For example, if you and the puppy go for a neighborhood walk and the puppy quits in mid-walk and refuses to go back, you've gone too far. The chart on p.132 has some ideas for activities you can do with your puppy at different ages.

■ **During physical exercise** *your puppy is also getting mental exercise. This stops her from becoming bored or destructive.*

Playtime should be fun

PLAYTIME CAN BE A PART of exercise, especially if you play retrieving games with your puppy, but playtime can also be separate from exercise. Playtime is fun, and this fun you and your puppy have together helps create the bond between you.

Play ideas for young puppies

Young puppies need their exercise in small doses:

a Roll your puppy over back and forth, rub her tummy, and let her squirm and flail her legs

b Play short, quick, retrieving games with different toys

c Play easy, short hide-and-seek games

Play ideas for older pups

Older pups can give (and take from you!) more time and energy in play-exercise:

■ **A tummy rub** *means play, exercise, bonding, and showing your dominance – all in one go.*

a Make the retrieving games a little longer

b Make the hide-and-seek games slightly more difficult, but still easily accomplishable

c Teach the puppy some fun tricks, like shake, roll over, or dance

d Teach the puppy the names of her toys, such as ball, bone, or squeaker

Don't wrestle with your puppy or play games like tug of war with her. This teaches her to fight you and to use her jaws and her strength against you. This is always a bad idea. Play games that require her cooperation instead.

SIMPLE EXERCISE IDEAS FOR YOUR PUPPY

8 to 12 weeks old

- A walk around the neighborhood
- A walk around the local park, harbor, shopping center, or school
- A short, easy hike in the local woods or meadow
- Throw the tennis ball (in short throws)

■ **Walking** *is one of the best exercises for dogs – and for humans!*

12 to 18 weeks old

- Slightly longer walks
- Very short jogs on a soft surface, such as grass
- Climbing sessions on playground equipment
- Slightly longer hikes in the woods or other wild lands

■ **Activity on playground** *equipment needs to be carefully assisted and supervised.*

Older puppies

- For the more athletic breeds, introduce them to your bicycle and very gradually start teaching them to run alongside the bike
- Very gradually increase the distance and speed of walks
- Very gradually increase the distance and speed of jogs

■ **Running** *after a bicycle exercises your pup while giving her the satisfaction and joy of a good chase.*

Spaying and neutering

MOST DOGS SHOULD BE SPAYED, *if female, or neutered, if male, (see box below). The only dogs that should be bred are those that are the best representatives of their breed in physical conformation, temperament, genetic health, and working characteristics.*

Unwanted dogs

Unfortunately, this selective breeding hasn't been the case for much of our history, and the end result has been hundreds of thousands of dogs born only to be destroyed. Some are killed because there aren't enough homes available, others because of health or temperament problems.

Each dog that is given up as unwanted, or becomes a stray, or is involved in a dog bite situation, ends up costing taxpayers money. Because of this, many cities are trying to regulate dog breeding. Many have instituted fines or costly licenses to try to discourage dog breeding. These measures may inconvenience the reputable, responsible breeder but unfortunately won't do anything to control accidental indiscriminate, breedings. This is where spaying and neutering come in.

A spayed or neutered dog cannot reproduce, even accidentally!

SPAYING AND NEUTERING

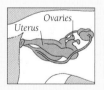  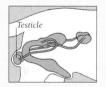

Ovaries
Uterus

BEFORE SPAYING   AFTER SPAYING   Testicle   BEFORE NEUTERING   AFTER NEUTERING

 Spaying

Spaying a female dog consists of a surgical ovario-hysterectomy. The ovaries and uterus are removed through an incision in the abdomen.

b **Neutering**

Neutering a male dog consists of removing his testicles through an incision made just in front of the scrotum.

What age?

Traditionally, dogs have been spayed or neutered at about 6 months of age. However, in an effort to discourage breeding, many humane societies have been spaying and neutering very young puppies – some as young as 8 weeks of age.

Surgery at the age of 8 weeks has so far been shown to have no ill effects on a puppy's health, and early spay/neuter programs have been very successful.

Taking care

After your female puppy is spayed, your veterinarian will tell you to keep her quiet for a few days. Most dogs don't show any signs of discomfort and recuperate very quickly. Her stitches will come out in about 10 days. A female that has been spayed will not go through her "heat season," ending that twice-a-year hassle. She will not spot your floors and carpets, and male dogs will no longer come calling!

For a neutered male puppy, again your vet will tell you to keep him quiet for a few days, but that could be difficult because the puppy won't appear to be uncomfortable at all.

The benefits

While stopping unwanted reproduction is a powerful reason to spay or neuter your dog, there are many other health benefits as well:

For males:

In a male dog, neutering will:

- Decrease male sexual behaviors, including leg-lifting, marking, roaming and fighting
- Decrease the desire to escape from the yard
- Decrease the incidence of fights
- Protect him from testicular cancer
- Decrease the tendency towards problem aggressive behavior without affecting the dog's working ability

■ **Neutering your dog** *will not affect his health or useful aspects of his personality, such as his protectiveness toward his territory (your house), and you.*

DON'T WORRY ABOUT...

1 ... your spayed or neutered dog getting fat. This is a myth. Too much food and not enough exercise make dogs fat!

2 ... your spayed or neutered dog missing sex. This does not happen. Dogs don't make love as part of a complex relationship, they copulate as a response to biological urges. Remove the biological urges, and they'll never think about sex again. It's really that simple

For females:

In a female dog, spaying will:

- Decrease the incidence of breast cancers
- Protect her against cancers of the reproductive system
- Decrease the incidence of female aggression

Working with your vet

IN THE PREVIOUS CHAPTER, *I talked about your puppy's first visit to the vet. But your relationship with the vet should not stop there. You need to continue to work with your veterinarian to keep your puppy healthy.*

Some puppy owners seem to begrudge the money spent at the veterinarian's office. They think that every time the veterinarian suggests a regular check-up or an office visit, he's just out to get their money. Certainly the vet needs to earn a living, just as you and I do. However, your vet is also dedicated to maintaining your puppy's good health. Let him help.

■ **Don't remember your vet** *only in times of crisis. Take your puppy to him for check-ups and advice on preventing problems. This will be more cost-effective in the long run!*

RECOGNIZING HEALTH PROBLEMS

Many healthy puppies grow up to be healthy adults that see the vet once a year for booster vaccines. For a dog that never shows signs of any health problems, this is fine. But what if your puppy develops health problems? Recognizing those problems is important, because catching one early on may save you, your puppy, and your vet considerable grief. Call your vet if you notice any of these problems:

1. Vomiting that doesn't stop after a couple of hours

2. Diarrhea that continues more than one day, or that contains a lot of mucus or any blood

3. A temperature lower than 101°F or above 102.5°F

4. Fainting, collapse, or a seizure

5. A severe cough, trouble breathing, or a suspected obstruction

6. The puppy refuses to eat and misses more than two meals

7. A leg that is obviously hurt, with no weight put on it, and is still held up after a gentle massage

8. A distended or tender abdomen

9. Any eye injury

10. Heavy breathing for no apparent reason

11. Potential allergic reactions, such as swelling, hives, or rashes, especially around the face

12. Potential poisoning, especially antifreeze, insecticides or herbicides, rodent or snail poison

13. Cuts or wounds that are bleeding and gape open, or do not stop bleeding with direct pressure

14. Suspected snake bites

15. The puppy is hiding and doesn't want to come out

16. Panting other than after exercise or playtime

17. Lack of energy

18. Restlessness for no apparent reason

Never ignore the trouble signs, hoping they will go away. They may, but then again, they may not. That wasted time could make a health problem much worse for your puppy.

What your vet will want to know

When you call your veterinarian, the receptionist will ask you several questions. It is her job to get as much information as possible and pass it on to the vet. She will then talk to the vet and have some answers or advice for you, or the vet will get on the line to talk to you.

Probable questions

Be prepared to answer these queries:

1 What is the specific problem?

2 What made you notice it? What are the symptoms?

3 What is the puppy's temperature?

4 Has the puppy eaten? When? What? How much?

5 Is there any vomiting? Diarrhea? What does it look like?

6 Has the puppy been anywhere or done anything that might have caused this problem or affected her in some way?

7 How long has this problem been going on?

■ **Your vet's receptionist** *helps you by gathering information and organizing it properly for the vet. Assist her by being patient and not insisting on talking to the vet yourself.*

Give your veterinarian more information rather than less. Let him wade through the information and decide what is relevant and what isn't – that's where his expertise comes into play. Your job is to supply him with enough information so that he can help you and your puppy.

■ **Indulge your puppy** *when she is sick. Let her rest where she likes, keep her warm, and give her extra attention – but be sure to train her back to the usual routine once she's better.*

Treating your puppy at home

IMAGINE TRYING TO GET *your squirmy little puppy to swallow a pill!*
Giving your puppy medication isn't always easy, but there are some tricks to
make it easier. If at all possible, keep this experience as stress-free as possible.
If your puppy learns to hate medication and treatments now, as a puppy, she will
retain that hatred throughout her life – and that could be very difficult.

Giving liquid medicine

Liquid medication can be difficult and messy to administer.
Ask your vet for a few large syringes without needles. The
medication can be measured into the syringe. Then gently
place the tip of the syringe in the side of your puppy's
mouth, between the back teeth, and squirt the medicine
in carefully. When giving liquid medication, don't try
to force the puppy's mouth open. The medication will
end up all over you and her.

■ **Give the medicine** *a little at a*
time. Your pup can't swallow too fast.

Tablets and capsules

Pills, tablets, and capsules are actually easier to administer. Hide the medicine in a bit of
food – bits of hot dog, peanut butter, sliced cheese, and commercial dog treats are good
for this – and let your puppy eat it. To get my dogs to take their pills, I make a peanut
butter sandwich. One slice of bread is spread with the peanut butter and folded in half,
sandwiching the pill inside. I tear it into three pieces and offer the first two pieces
without the pill. The dog is therefore anticipating the treat and is no longer suspicious
about a pill. I then offer the last piece with the pill inside it. One swallow and it's gone!

Eye and ear medicine

Take a spoonful of peanut butter and scrape it off on the roof of the puppy's mouth
behind the front teeth. As your puppy licks this and tries to swallow it, gently hold
her head and apply the medication. For eye medication, be sure and
swift or your pup will get nervous. For ear medication, gently wipe
out her ear with a cotton ball first.

Follow your vet's directions for all medications. If a medicine is to
be given three times a day for 10 days, then give it three times a day
for 10 days. Anything more or less could endanger your pup's health.

■ **Eye medication** *should be sure and swift otherwise the puppy will get nervous.*

■ **Ear medicine** *is easy to administer with a dropper or syringe.*

Common sense

Much of this medication may not be necessary if you puppy-proof your house and take reasonable care. Make sure anything poisonous is put away where your puppy cannot reach it. Put latches on cupboard doors. Make sure the trash is unreachable. Do car repairs where she cannot get into the stuff you use.

Don't let your puppy near oil, grease, gasoline, or antifreeze. Just a lick or two of antifreeze is enough to kill your puppy.

Don't let her play off leash if there are cars nearby. Examine her for things that may have stuck to her coat when she was playing outdoors. Common sense will go a long way in keeping your puppy in good health.

A simple summary

✔ Exercise and playtime use up your puppy's energy and develop strength and coordination.

✔ Spaying or neutering helps avoid unneeded pups, reduces unwanted sexual behaviors, and benefits your puppy's health.

✔ Your veterinarian helps you keep your pup healthy.

✔ Use common sense to avoid accidents.

Chapter 11

Routine Care From Tip to Tail

Y OUR PUPPY CANNOT CARE for himself, so it's up to you to do it for him. No matter what breed he is or what kind of coat he has, he will need regular grooming: his toenails trimmed and his teeth brushed (if you think only a simpleton would brush his dog's teeth, read on!), and checks for fleas, burrs, or tangled hair. Grooming and body care for your puppy is like regular maintenance on your car – it's vital and has to be done on schedule!

In this chapter:

✓ No getting around regular grooming

✓ Brushing your puppy

✓ Rub a dub dub a pup in the tub

✓ Trimming the toenails

✓ Ears and teeth

✓ The daily massage

GROOMING CAN BE A SHARED EXPERIENCE!

No getting around regular grooming

MANY DOG OWNERS BELIEVE only *Poodles and other breeds with long or curly hair need to be groomed. Not so! All dogs, regardless of breed and coat type, require some grooming. Some breeds, of course, like Poodles and Pekingese, do require more.*

It depends on the breed

Your puppy's breed (or mixture of breeds) and coat type will affect how much grooming he needs and what kind. The Poodles, Spaniels, and Schnauzers have hair that continues to grow all the time. Regular haircuts to keep their coat manageable are a must. In addition, this hair can gather into big mats if it is not combed regularly.

German Shepherd Dogs, Siberian Huskies, and Alaskan Malamutes have a thick double coat that sheds regularly, sometimes heavily. These dogs don't need a haircut, but need thorough brushing to pull out the dead undercoat and to keep the shedding manageable. Shorthaired dogs are not without their grooming needs. They can shed just as much as their longer-haired cousins; the hair they shed is just shorter. Shed short hair is not always easier to deal with, either.

Long dog hair tends to ball up, forming those infamous dog-hair dust bunnies. Short hair is prickly and sticks into things, including sofa cushions, pillows, and your clothes.

A professional groomer can help you

A *groomer* knows how to brush out coats, de-mat them (when possible), and what type of haircut each breed should have. Groomers also know about hair care products, including shampoos, conditioners, or special products such as de-matting conditioners and flea control preparations. They will also trim your dog's toenails on request, and some will even express the anal glands. Expect to pay extra for these services.

Trivia...

One spring many years ago my German Shepherd Dog, Watachie, was shedding heavily, so I took him outside to brush. I brushed and brushed and the grass became covered with his thick winter coat. When I sat down to rest my arm, I realized that birds were congregating around us, picking up his hair. A whole generation of baby birds was raised in nests lined with Watachie's winter coat!

DEFINITION

A **groomer** is a person whose career is caring for the skin and coat of dogs, cats, and other pets.

Getting your pup used to the groomer

You should introduce your puppy to the groomer and her salon when the puppy is between 10 and 12 weeks old, as soon as he has had at least two sets of shots. Don't take him before that, because he will be exposed to other dogs at the shop. Bring a few treats with you when you go to the shop, and encourage the receptionist, the groomer, and other staff members to give him treats, scratch his ears, pet him, and make a fuss over him. You want him to like going to the groomer.

On the second or third trip there, let the groomer put him up on the grooming table and comb or brush him. She can offer him a treat at the same time. Remember, you want this to be a positive experience, because he will be going there regularly.

Do not leave your puppy at the groomer for several hours until you have made at least three short visits with him. If he is frightened by being left there, subsequent visits will be traumatic.

A grooming routine

When your puppy goes to the grooming salon for the full treatment, his routine will probably go like this:

1. He will be thoroughly brushed

2. He will be bathed

3. He will be dried, in a dryer cage or with a handheld dryer

4. He will be brushed again

5. He will get his hair cut or trimmed

6. He will get the final brushing and any final trims or touch-ups

■ **A professional groomer** *is better equipped and qualified to give your puppy special clipping. Grooming for good looks is not only about prettiness but also about not hurting the dog, or harming his skin.*

143

Grooming tools

Grooming tools come in a variety of sizes, shapes, and uses. Some are right for certain hair types and not for others. It's important to know what tools are correct for your puppy's coat.

Combs

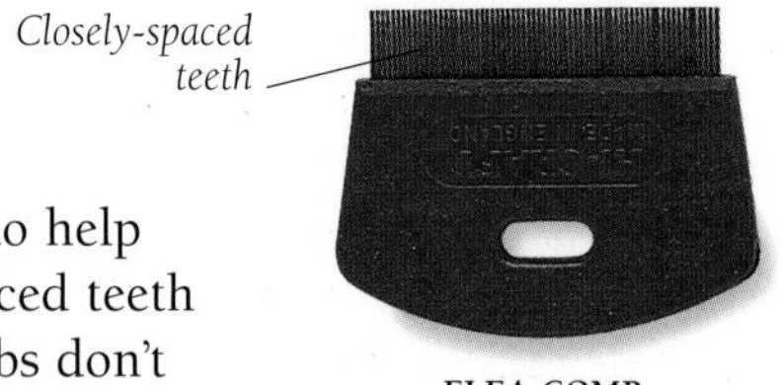

Combs are used to go through a coat to smooth it, or to help remove small tangles. Most are metal, with closely-spaced teeth on one side and wider spaced teeth on the other. Combs don't have much value on shorthaired dogs or dogs with very thick, dense undercoats, but will work on dogs with fine hair or medium-dense coats.

Closely-spaced teeth

FLEA COMB

A flea comb (shown here) has very fine, closely spaced teeth that drag fleas out of the coat. It works well on shorthaired dogs, as well as medium and fine-haired dogs.

PROFESSIONAL GROOMERS SUGGEST...

If you have any questions about which tools to use or how to use them, make an appointment with your local groomer. Ask her to show you the correct way to use the tools on your puppy, and expect to pay her for her time. Meanwhile, these are the standard grooming tools used for different breeds:

Cocker Spaniels
A de-matter for longer hair, especially if it's tangled; a slicker brush for areas with shorter hair, especially if the dog has had a haircut; and a pin brush.

Rottweilers
A natural bristle brush, even one made for people.

German Shepherd Dogs
A pin brush; a slicker brush; and a de-matter for the heavy undercoat.

Poodles
A pin brush; a slicker brush; a metal comb; and a de-matter.

Silky and Yorkshire Terriers,
A de-matter; a metal comb; and a pin brush.

Golden Retrievers
A de-matter; a pin brush; and a metal comb.

Labrador Retrievers
A natural bristle brush; and a slicker brush.

Australian Shepherds
A pin brush and a de-matter.

Shih Tzu and Lhasa Apsos
A de-matter; a metal comb; a pin brush.

Brushes

Various kinds of dog brushes are available:

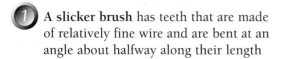 **A slicker brush** has teeth that are made of relatively fine wire and are bent at an angle about halfway along their length

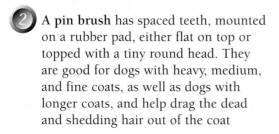 **A pin brush** has spaced teeth, mounted on a rubber pad, either flat on top or topped with a tiny round head. They are good for dogs with heavy, medium, and fine coats, as well as dogs with longer coats, and help drag the dead and shedding hair out of the coat

■ **A slicker brush** *is good for the top coat, but does not reach deep into a long or thick coat.*

3 **A de-matter** brush has three, four, or five blades, usually about an inch and a half long, that are sharp on one side. These brushes are for the thick hair around the dog's neck and the back of the legs. They rake through the thick, dense coat, splitting any tangles or mats. They will also drag out any dead or shedding coat

4 **A rake** has four to six short metal teeth set in a row. Designed to find tangles and drag out dead hair, it's good for brushing a dense coat that isn't too long or dense

Brushing your puppy

SINCE GROOMING IS GOING *to be a regular part of your puppy's routine care, you want him to enjoy it. If he sees the brush and comes to you wagging his tail with joy, half your job is already done. But if he runs away when he see the brush, grooming is going to be a hated chore all his life, and a struggle for you both.*

Short and sweet

To teach your puppy to enjoy grooming, have some special treats on hand and keep the session very short. For my dogs, peanut butter is the special treat. I give a puppy a fingerful of peanut butter, brush one side or one leg, and then let the puppy go, praising him, "Good puppy! Yeah! Such a special boy!" The grooming session is then tolerable, quick, and full of rewards. As the puppy learns to enjoy it, I make the sessions a little bit longer – very gradually – and continue the rewards.

Rub a dub dub, a pup in the tub

THE OLD WIVES' TALES say
*a dog should only be bathed once a
year, or once in the spring and once
in the fall. Obviously those dogs lived
outside. They were never allowed in
the house because they stank! It doesn't
hurt your puppy at all to be bathed
more often, as long as you use a
good quality shampoo and rinse
it out thoroughly.*

■ **Bathe your pup indoors** *and make the first
few baths pleasant. Don't bathe him using cold
water from the garden hose – that will just teach
him to hate baths. Later, when he's grown up, you
can bathe him under the hose in warm weather.*

Doggy shampoo

There are a thousand dog shampoos available commercially, and all are good for some
dogs. Read the labels and make sure the shampoo you buy is recommended for puppies.
Don't get a medicated shampoo unless your veterinarian recommends it. Don't use an
insecticide shampoo either unless it is specifically for puppies and your puppy actually
has fleas. Instead, get a good quality shampoo that is just made for cleaning the puppy.

*Shampoos made for people are not good for puppies. Our
hair and skin just isn't the same. People shampoos dry out
a puppy's skin.*

Towel   Doggy   Non-skid
        shampoo   mat

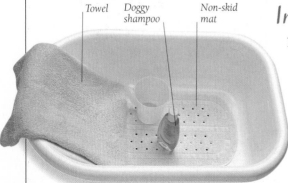

Into the tub

I wash my puppies in the bathtub. I have a
handheld shower nozzle (a massager type)
and non-skid patches on the bottom of the tub.
If you have a deep sink in the garage or basement,
that might also work.

■ **Keep your towels** *and the shampoo within
reach before you put your puppy in the tub.*

GETTING READY FOR HIS BATH

Brush or comb your puppy thoroughly before you bathe him. Make sure all the tangles are out of his coat, because if they're not, you'll have to cut them out after the bath. Water turns tangles into cement! Put a cotton ball into each of his ears to help keep the ears dry. Set the water to a nice comfortable temperature (it should just feel warm on your hand) and lift the puppy in.

1 Wetting

Use a mug, or a handheld shower, to thoroughly wet your puppy. If he struggles, calm him with your voice but remember, you must not let him fight you.

2 Lathering

Work the shampoo into his coat, from the neck backward. Take care to keep the shampoo out of his eyes. Watch out, he will shake his head!

3 Rinsing

Rinse him off. On his head, run the water away from his eyes and ears. Don't stint on the water; make sure all the soap is rinsed out.

4 Drying

Dry him thoroughly before he shakes the water off himself vigorously, giving you an impromptu bath!

SPECIAL CLEANING – IT'S SIMPLE!

To clean out	What you can do
● Fleas	A flea comb will catch some of the little pests, especially around the puppy's eyes and ears. Insecticides also work, but many owners are afraid of using too much, and it's a very real concern. Only use flea and tick preparations made especially for puppies. If you have any doubts or concerns, consult with your veterinarian. Talk to your veterinarian about his recommendations for flea control. There are many options available these days (Chapter 13 discusses several of them).
● Gum and other sticky stuff	Rub the area with ice to freeze the gum and break it out, or pour on some vegetable oil to ooze it out. (Follow up the oil treatment with a bath). However, be aware that gum usually needs to be trimmed out.
● Paint	Don't use paint solvents on your puppy. They're toxic! Try to wash the paint out with soap and water. If it won't come out, trim away the painted hair.
● Motor oil	A simple detergent dishwashing soap usually cuts the oil. Just make sure you rinse it out well.
● Burrs, foxtails, and other seed	Many seeds can simply be combed out. If they're stuck in a tangle, use some vegetable oil (just a little) or some hair conditioner to make the burr a little slippery. You will then have to wash the oil or conditioner out with a good shampoo. If the seed has really worked into the coat, trim it out.
● Quills and spines	Call your veterinarian. Pulling out or working out quills can be very painful, and your vet may want to sedate the dog while he does it.
● Skunks	Soak your dog in tomato juice or vinegar, rubbing it deep into the coat. Let it sit for a few minutes, then rinse it out. You may need to repeat the treatment several times. A simple detergent dishwashing soap also helps cut the smell (it cleans out the oil in the skunk's discharge). There are also commercial preparations on the market that will do.

Trimming the terrible toenails

MOST DOG OWNERS hate trimming their dog's toenails, but letting the nails grow too long can actually cause the dog pain and, over time, can deform the feet. It's time to cut your puppy's nails when your puppy is standing still, upright on all four paws, and his nails touch the floor. Learn to trim your puppy's toenails while he is still young and his nails are soft.

Step-by-step trimming

Trimming is simple if you use the correct tools, keep a treat at hand, and act gentle but sure. Use special "guillotine cutters" which have short, curved blades.

1. With your puppy busy with peanut butter, lying in your lap such that you can see his feet, check his toes.

■ **If you do it right,** *trimming your puppy's nails should merely be a bit of a yawn (at least for the puppy)!*

2. Push the hair away from the nail. If the nail is clear or white, you will be able to see the pink quick inside. The nail beyond it has no feeling at all – just like your nails. This is where you should cut.

3. If there are no white nails, you will just have to practice and guess a little. When you look at a toenail from the side, you will see it curves out and down. The last third of the nail is much narrower and comes to a point. It is always safe to trim off that last third of the nail.

4. If your puppy has black nails, check all of his toes. If he has one white nail, that will give you some idea about where the quick is, and you can cut the black nails slightly longer than the white one.

DEFINITION

Quick

Cut here

The **quick** is a bundle of nerves and bloods vessels inside the nail.

If you cut the quick while trimming your puppy's nails, scrape the nail along a bar of soap. The soft soap will clog the nail until the blood can clot. Keep the puppy on your lap with his foot up for a few minutes, until the bleeding stops.

Ears and teeth

CLEANING YOUR PUPPY'S EARS AND TEETH *is nowhere near as difficult as trimming toenails. For one thing, there's no chance of making him bleed. If you think it's crazy to brush a dog's teeth, ask yourself why you brush yours. Isn't is healthy for you? Doesn't your dog deserve the same consideration?*

Cleaning the ears

While cleaning his ears, wet a cotton ball with witch hazel, alcohol, or commercial canine ear-cleaning solution and wring out most of the moisture. With your puppy on your lap and distracted by a lick of peanut butter, lift the ear flap and gently wipe the creases. If the ear is dirty, you may need two or three cotton balls.

Cleaning the ears

Get a very small child's toothbrush for your dog, or buy one specially designed for dogs. Ask your vet or the local pet supply store for canine toothpaste. If you use this, your pup will not need to rinse his mouth. Or you may use baking soda.

Don't use your toothpaste on your puppy. Not all of the ingredients are safe for dogs, and the taste is offensive to canines.

Invite your puppy to lie down in your lap, and open his lips with your fingers. You obviously can't use peanut butter to distract him in this case, so be gentle and speak soothingly to him if he gets restive. Start by gently rubbing the toothbrush up against the outside of his side teeth. He will probably try to chew on the brush. If he does, take the brush away as you gently discourage him. Then try it again.

■ **Do not try** *to clean deep within your puppy's ear canal – just clean the easily-reachable areas.*

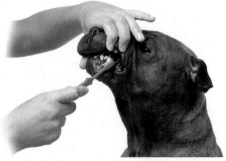

■ **A clean mouth** *is less likely to be diseased and cause diseases in your puppy.*

The daily massage

IT'S IMPORTANT TO KNOW *your puppy's body very well. You need to know what is normal and what isn't. Your puppy often cannot tell you when there's a problem. Sure, he can cry or limp when he hurts his paw, but how can he tell you when he has an unusual lump on his side? He can't.*

INTERNET

www.healthypet.com

This site, maintained by the American Animal Hospital Association, includes pet care tips and a library.

The easiest and most enjoyable way to examine your puppy is to give him a massage.

You'll both love it

I like to massage-cum-examine my dogs in the evening when the television is on. I sit on the floor, with my dog lying in front of me, on his side. I start at his head and gently feel his muzzle. I peek in at his teeth, look at his nose and eyes, and rub the base of his ears as I look inside each ear. I massage his neck all around, feeling for lumps, bumps, or seeds. I work down to the shoulders, the chest, down each front leg to the paws, and check each paw. I continue this thorough massage and examination until I have gone over his entire body.

A simple summary

✔ A groomer can be of great help to you in the grooming of your puppy and in assisting you with problems about grooming.

✔ Brushing, combing, and bathing your puppy do not have to be stressful activities. Introduce your puppy to these routines easily and gently, and you'll do fine.

✔ Trimming toenails, cleaning ears, and brushing teeth are all vital parts of the grooming routine.

✔ Never make a grooming task into a battle of wills. Be patient with your puppy, and give him lots of praise when he is well-behaved.

✔ A daily massage keeps you aware of your puppy's body and health.

Chapter 12

Let's Eat!

EVERYBODY – HUMAN, CANINE, OR REPTILIAN – needs good nutrition. What constitutes good nutrition depends upon the body being nourished. What is good nutrition now will not be the same when your puppy is an adult, or later when she is an old dog. Right now she needs a diet that fulfills all of her nutritional needs so that she can grow and remain healthy, while having enough energy left for exercise and play.

In this chapter:

✓ Commercial puppy foods

✓ What about supplements?

✓ Are preservatives safe?

✓ Puppy treats

✓ When should she eat?

✓ How much is enough?

■ **A good puppy food** *will address all the dietary requirements of your growing puppy.*

Commercial puppy foods

COMMERCIAL PUPPY FOODS *are designed to supply all of your puppy's nutritional needs, including proteins, amino acids, enzymes, fats, carbohydrates, vitamins, and minerals. Many of the companies that produce dog foods use feeding trials to test their foods. These companies have fed, literally, generations upon generations of dogs. However, all dog (and puppy) foods are not created equal.*

You get what you pay for

Dog food is one item where you usually get what you pay for. The more expensive puppy foods are – as a general rule – better quality foods. The less expensive foods – especially the generic or plain label foods – are lesser quality foods.

Quality can be based on many things, including testing. Feeding trials are not required for a company to market pet food. Instead of trials, companies can use laboratory tests to determine the nutritional value of a food. Unfortunately, lab tests are not as good as feeding trials, because they don't measure the food as it is actually used or metabolized by the puppy. Therefore, a dog food could test well in the laboratory but still not adequately nourish your puppy. Foods that are tested by actually feeding dogs (feeding trials) will say so on the label of the dog food.

DRY OR WET?

There are three main types of dog food:

DRY FOOD

1 **Dry, kibbled foods**

These come in a bag and are broken up into small pieces. They usually contain grains and meats. Dry foods have a good shelf life and most dogs eat them quite readily. They are usually very affordable – some more so than others.

Ingredients

The quality of a pet food is also based on the quality of the ingredients. Grains grown in mineral-poor soils will have few minerals to pass on to the puppy that consumes them. Poor-quality meats will be less able to nourish the puppy. Less expensive foods contain inexpensive and less nourishing grains and less of the more expensive meats. Again, the puppy's nutrition can, and often will, suffer.

What about preservatives?

Many dog owners are also concerned about the preservatives, artificial flavorings, and additives in many dog foods. Some of these additives are of questionable value as far as your puppy's nutrition is concerned.

If you have a concern about a particular additive or ingredient, call your veterinarian and the manufacturer of the food.

> ### Trivia...
> *Plain label dog foods are inexpensive to buy but expensive in other ways. The University of California at Davis Veterinary College has named a malnutrition syndrome found in dogs fed a poor quality food: generic dog food disease.*

SEMI-MOIST FOOD

Meat chunks in gravy

Meat chunks in jelly

MEATY CANNED FOOD

2 Semi-moist foods

These have a higher moisture content than dry, kibbled foods, but not as high as canned. Many dog treats are semi-moist. These foods are high in sugar and salt, as well as artificial colorings – none of which your puppy really needs.

3 Wet, canned foods

These are mostly meats or meat recipes. They have a high water content. In the can they have a long shelf life, but once the can is opened they must be used right away. Canned foods are very palatable but are more expensive than dry foods.

Reading the label

The label on each bag (or can) of dog food will tell you a lot about that food. One section of the label lists the percentages of nutrients. Most puppies do well on a food that contains about 28 percent protein and 8 percent fat. The label will also tell you the ingredients of the food, listed in quantity order. In other words, the first ingredient listed will be what the food has the most of. Therefore, if beef is listed first, followed by rice, corn, and wheat, you'll know that there is more beef in the food than rice, and more rice than corn.

However, this listing can be deceptive. You might see wheat midlings, wheat germ, and wheat bran listed in a food, all listed after the meat ingredient. Since they are listed after the meat, does that mean there is more meat than wheat? Not necessarily. There might be more meat than wheat midlings, or more meat than wheat germ. But if all the wheat is added together, there might very well be more wheat than meat. You need to read the label carefully so you know exactly what you are feeding your puppy.

FROM THE HORSE'S MOUTH...

Pet food company web sites usually list the ingredients that are in their foods, and other important information. They often give general information on care and nutrition, too. Here is a selection of dog food manufacturers' phone numbers and web sites:

Nutro Products
(800) 833-5330
www.nutroproducts.com

Purina
(800) 778-7462
www.purina.com

Pedigree
(800) 525-5273
www.pedigree.com

Canidae Pet Foods
(800) 398-1600
www.canidae.com

Wysong Corp.
(517) 6310009
www.wysong.net

Nature's Recipe
800-237-3856
www.naturesrecipe.
heinzpetproducts.com

Friskies
[The makers of Alpo and Mighty Dog]
(800) 551-7392
www.friskies.com

Hill's Pet Nutrition, Inc.
[The makers of Science Diet]
(800) 255-2403
www.hillspet.com

Iams Co.
[The makers of Iams and Eukanuba]
(800) 863-4267
www.iamsco.com

Ingredient lists are very important if your puppy develops allergies. Many dogs are allergic to wheat, for example, and their owners must read labels very carefully.

Which is the best form for your puppy? Most veterinarians and breeders recommend dry food. The action of chewing the hard kibble will help keep your dog's teeth clean and healthy. And dry foods provide the most nutrients for the money. Since wet foods are mostly water, your dog has to eat a lot more of them in order to get the nutrition she needs every day. That means more going in, and more coming out by the puppy – which may not be very good news for your housetraining program!

Picking a food

Choosing the right food for your puppy can be difficult. If you have any questions about the food, talk to your veterinarian and call the food manufacturer. Here are some suggestions to help you decide when you read the ingredients:

(a) Is there a good variety of foods?

(b) Are there complete and incomplete proteins?

(c) Is there a selection of carbohydrates and fats?

(d) What about additives and preservatives? Do you understand what they are and why they are in the food?

(e) What are the protein and fat percentages? Are you comfortable with those levels in your puppy's diet?

Monitor your puppy

The general growth and personality of your puppy should be your guide regarding the food you give her:

- Is she growing well?
- Is she too skinny?
- Is she too fat?
- Does she always act hungry?
- Does she have enough energy for play?

■ **The final, and best, test** *of a dog food is the response of the puppy who eats it. If your pup is thriving the food is probably fine.*

What about supplements?

MOST EXPERTS AGREE that a good quality commercial puppy food contains everything a puppy needs. However, many people are still tempted to supplement their puppy's diet. Perhaps you take vitamin and mineral supplements yourself, and think your dog needs them too.

Vitamins and minerals

The first thing to remember is that a good quality dog food is probably a lot healthier than the food you eat. It has been carefully tested and balanced for optimum nutrition, and most of us don't do that with our daily meals. Still, if you want to give your puppy extra vitamins and minerals, it probably won't do her any harm.

BONEMEAL

CALCIUM TABLETS

VITAMIN TABLETS

Most dog food manufacturers confirm that as long as the supplements do not exceed 10 percent of the food fed, they probably will not disturb the nutritional balance of the commercial food. Just make sure you follow the manufacturer's directions. More is not better with many vitamins and minerals; excessive amounts of some can cause serious problems.

Other foods

Many dog owners also add other kinds of supplements, such as yogurt and brewer's yeast, to their dog's diet. Yogurt has been said to aid digestion by adding beneficial bacteria to the digestive tract. It's nutritious and a good source of fat, and certainly will not hurt your puppy unless she has trouble digesting dairy products. As for brewer's yeast, many dog owners believe it will naturally repel fleas. This has never been proven, but yeast is a food source of B vitamins, and again, it will not hurt the dog when used as a supplement.

Vegetables, vegetable juice, or meat broth can be added to your dog's dry food. They add nutrition and make the food more palatable. Cooked eggs, cheese, or cottage cheese can also make dry food more attractive.

Too much supplementation can upset a previously balanced and complete diet. Supplement carefully, and if you have any doubts, talk to your veterinarian.

Are preservatives safe?

MOST COMMERCIAL DOG FOODS *contain preservatives to help extend their shelf life. Most preservatives, like ethoxyquin or the tocopherols, are antioxidants – they prevent the oxidation of fatty acids and vitamins. However, some preservatives have been linked with health problems.*

Ethoxyquin

The most controversial preservative currently used in dog food is ethoxyquin, a chemical that prevents the fats in food from losing their potency. Approved by the Food and Drug Administration for use in human food, ethoxyquin has been alleged to have caused cancer, and liver, kidney, and thyroid problems. However, this has never been proven.

If you are worried about ethoxyquin, use dog food preserved with tocopherols – antioxidants that are naturally occurring compounds of vitamins C and E. Be aware that these have a very short shelf life.

PUPPY TREATS

Any treat you feed your puppy, whether as part of a training regimen or to keep her busy with a toy, must be taken into account when considering her overall diet. If you use treats as part of a training program, measure out a proportion of treats for the day, and minus some dog food from your puppy's daily ration to compensate. There are many brands of commercial treats in the market. Some are pure junk food, full of corn syrup, meat scraps, and sugar, while others are good nutrition. Here are some treat ideas:

- Bits of meat or cheese make good training treats
- A carrot makes a good chew treat
- A slice of apple is a much better sweet treat than a commercial treat containing sugar and artificial colors
- Of the commercial products, the hard biscuit-type treats are probably best. They have fewer artificial colors, additives, and flavors, and less sugar than semi-moist treats

Never treat your dog with chocolate. It's lethal to dogs. A 10-ounce milk chocolate candy bar can kill a 7-pound dog.

When should she eat?

MOST YOUNG PUPPIES NEED to eat three times a day. A big morning meal, a small lunch, and a big evening meal usually suit 8- to 12-week-old puppies just fine. By 12 weeks of age, most puppies will be able to skip lunch and do quite well with just morning and evening meals. That doesn't mean you should start feeding them less. It just means that you can divide their daily ration into two servings a day instead of three.

By 14 to 18 months of age, most young dogs will eat one or two meals a day, and usually indicate by preference how often and what time of day they are more comfortable eating. Some dogs will simply stop eating their morning meal and will eagerly consume the evening meal, while others will do just the opposite. If your dog has a hearty appetite at both meals, that's OK too. Two meals a day is fine for an adult dog.

No free feeding

Free feeding is not a good idea, for several reasons. Food that is set out for free feeding is easily spoiled. Ants, flies, and other insects can soil it; rodents can visit it; and heat can spoil it.

DEFINITION

Free feeding *means leaving food out for your puppy to nibble on all day.*

If your puppy does happen to get sick, one of the first questions the veterinarian will ask is, "How is your puppy's appetite? How did she eat this morning?" If the puppy eats sporadically throughout the day rather than at specific times, you won't be able to answer that question.

Housetraining is much easier when the puppy eats at specific times.

You know she needs to go outside after every meal. If those meals are at set times, you know when to take her outside. However, if the puppy snacks all day, when should you take her out? It's much harder to tell.

■ **Feeding at set times** *enhances the relationship between you and your pup. As the giver of the food, you assume an important position in her life.*

How much is enough?

THE LABEL ON THE DOG FOOD you buy will have recommendations
for how much to feed your puppy. They are a good place to start, but don't take
them as the final word. Every puppy is different, and the amount of exercise
your pup has had, how cold it is outside, and lots of other factors will affect
how much your puppy should eat.

Watch your puppy

Regulate how much you feed your puppy by how she looks and feels. If she is thin
and is always acting hungry, give her some more food. If she is fat and doesn't always
seem interested in mealtimes, cut back. If she is sleek and active and growing
well, you've got it just right. Along the same lines, if she has been working
hard, give her a little extra, and if she has spent the day lying around, cut
back a bit.

*If your puppy is healthy and growing well, don't force her to eat
more than she wants.*

A simple summary

✓ A good quality food is important
to your puppy's growth and to
her continued good health.

✓ You get what you pay for with
puppy food, and the more
expensive brands are usually
the better ones.

✓ Dry foods are generally better for
your dog.

✓ Read the labels when making a
decision about which food to buy.

✓ Supplements and treats should
be fed sparingly, and only as part
of an overall plan for good
canine nutrition.

✓ Free feeding is not a good idea.
Feed your puppy only on a
regular schedule.

Chapter 13

Health Concerns

EXTERNAL AND INTERNAL PARASITES – fleas, ticks, mites, and worms – are uniquely suited to bug your dog. The fleas and mites that thrive on dogs greatly prefer a canine host to a human one, though that's not to say they won't take a nibble out of you. You should also be familiar with the diseases your puppy can be exposed to, especially those that can threaten his health. Hopefully, you'll never need this information but it's here for you if you do.

In this chapter:

✓ Fighting fleas

✓ Attacking ticks

✓ Mange and ringworm

✓ Internal parasites

✓ Dangerous diseases

THE GRASS IS GREENER WHEN YOUR PUPPY IS FREE OF PARASITES

Fighting fleas

A FLEA IS A SMALL, crescent-shaped, 6-legged insect with a big abdomen and a small head. It has flat sides so it can slip through hair with ease. When caught, it will pop under your fingernail like a tiny balloon. If that sounds gross, you obviously haven't dealt with too many fleas. Fleas cause dogs so much torment, it can be very satisfying to pop the little pests!

The damage they do

Fleas live by biting your dog and taking a drop or two of blood each time they bite. A heavy infestation can cause anemia from the blood loss, especially for small, young puppies. But the blood loss isn't the worst of it.

Fleas carry a wide variety of diseases. They are the intermediate host for tapeworms. If your dog has fleas and swallows an infected flea, he can then become infested with tapeworms.

Trivia...

Fleas can jump 6 feet in one hop. But despite their talents, most flea circuses (remember those?) never contained any live fleas. The so-called fleas were either dead and glued into place, or were so small they were invisible!

■ **Many dogs are allergic** *to flea bites, and scratch and chew themselves raw. This can result in dermatitis, or open sores, which could then develop secondary infections. Check your puppy's coat regularly for black, pepper-like matter which indicates fleas.*

Flea control has changed

In the past, insecticides and pesticides in the form of collars, dips, and sprays were the only products available, and you had to use those with caution. If you weren't careful, you could easily end up poisoning yourself and your dog before you killed off all the fleas. Luckily, in the last few years several products have been introduced to make flea control easier and safer.

New anti-flea products

The new products on the market attack fleas in two ways. Some kill adult fleas (which are the only ones that bite). Others are called insect growth regulators, and they stop the immature flea from developing or maturing. To be really effective, most of the newer flea-control products combine the insecticide with an insect growth regulator.

The new products are systemic, meaning they enter the dog's body systems, and generally come in tablets and liquids. The tablets release the product into the dog's bloodstream, where the flea ingests it every time it bites. The liquids are poured along the dog's neck and back, where they are absorbed into the dog's skin to repel fleas.

The triple attack

To control fleas, you must attack them in three ways: on the dog, in your house, and in your yard. Leave out any one of the three and your control efforts will not be successful. However, with the new products available, flea control is now possible. A few years ago, the battle was on-going, with the fleas often winning! Some control methods include:

1 **On your dog**
Use a systemic such as Program or Sentinel. Do not use insecticides on the dog, or flea collars, unless the labels on both products specify that it is safe to do so.

2 **In your house**
Use a spray with an insect growth regulator designed for inside use. If your house is infested, use a spray with a quick-kill ingredient as well as an insect growth regulator. Use all products according to directions.

3 **In your yard**
Use a spray designed for outside use that contains an insect growth regulator. Repeat the application according to directions.

Don't mix different flea-control products. It can be deadly. Read the labels carefully and follow the directions.

Attacking ticks

A TICK IS AN 8-LEGGED, oblong insect with a head that imbeds into the skin. Ticks feed on the host's blood and, when engorged, will drop off. Ticks, like fleas, are known carriers of disease.

Ticks and disease

In the United States, Rocky Mountain Spotted Fever was a concern for many years. This acutely infectious disease is characterized by muscular pain, high fever, and skin eruptions. It can be found all over western North America.

Rocky Mountain Spotted Fever is still a danger, but a new disease has emerged that is even more frightening. Lyme Disease affects dogs as well as people, and is transmitted primarily by ticks. A lingering fever and joint pain (sometimes quite severe) are characteristics of this disease.

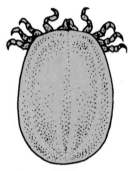

TICK

Ask your veterinarian if Lyme Disease is a problem in your area. If it is, there is a Lyme Disease vaccine. Ask your vet if he or she recommends it.

Nothing beats a hands-on exam

Although some flea products are partially effective on ticks, they are rarely totally effective at killing or keeping ticks off your dog. During tick season (spring and summer) you will have to examine your dog daily and remove each and every tick.

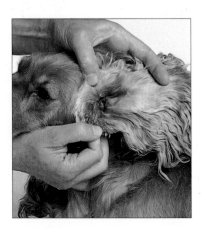

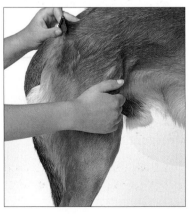

■ **The favorite hiding spots** *for ticks are in the ears (or behind them) and around the neck. Another commonly affected area is the "armpit" area of the legs. However, you should check your puppy all over for ticks, during tick season.*

Grab the tick down close to the skin and pull gently but firmly, with a slow, twisting motion. Don't flush the tick down the toilet – it will survive its trip downstream. And don't squish it between your fingers, because you will be exposed to whatever diseases it is carrying. The best way to kill a tick is to burn it. Put a little antibiotic ointment on the wound where the tick was embedded.

Never remove a tick with your bare fingers. Use tweezers or wear rubber gloves.

Mange and ringworm

MANGE IS USUALLY ASSOCIATED *with stray dogs, but this isn't necessarily so. Many well-cared for dogs have come down with mange too. Ringworm is highly contagious and can infect people as well as other pets.*

Kinds of mange

There are two types of mange seen most often in dogs:

1. **Sarcoptic mange** is contagious to people and other pets. Its primary symptoms include red welts that the dog will be scratching continuously. Sarcoptic mange usually responds well to medical treatment.

2. **Demodectic mange** is not as easily transmitted to people or other pets. It shows up as bald patches, usually first on the dog's face. There may not be any scratching or itching. Demodectic mange often appears in young dogs and will clear up with treatment. However, in older dogs treatment can be long and drawn out, and is sometimes not effective at all.

Mange is a case for your veterinarian. Don't try to treat it yourself.

Ringworm

Ringworm isn't really a worm at all, but instead is several different kinds of fungi. These very contagious fungi infest the skin and cause ring-shaped, round, scaly, itchy spots. These round spots are the trademark identification of ringworm.

Ringworm usually responds well to veterinary treatment, but care must be taken to strictly follow the treatment plan set up by your veterinarian.

Internal parasites

INTERNAL PARASITES *are just as disgusting as external parasites, but can be more threatening to your dog's health because they are not as easily seen. You will see fleas on your dog, for example, but he could have worms for quite a while before you see any signs of poor health.*

Roundworms

Most puppies must be treated for roundworms. These long, white worms are fairly common in puppies, although they can also be found in adult dogs and humans, as well as other animals. A roundworm infestation in an adult dog is not always dangerous, especially if it is a light infestation. However, a heavy infestation can threaten a young dog's health.

■ **If your puppy licks** *his anal region, it may be a sign of worms.*

A young puppy with roundworms will not thrive and will appear thin, with a dull coat and a pot belly. Often you will see worms in the stool. Roundworms can be detected by your veterinarian through a fecal analysis. Good sanitation is important to prevent an infestation. Feces should be picked up and disposed of daily.

Roundworm eggs can be picked up via the feces, so your puppy should be discouraged from sniffing other dogs' feces.

Whipworms

These worms live in the large intestine, where they feed on blood. The eggs are passed in the feces, and can live in the soil for a long time – years, even. A dog that eats the fresh spring grass or buries his bone in the infected soil can pick up eggs.

If you garden, be careful, because you can pick up whipworm eggs under your nails.

Hookworms

Hookworms live in the small intestine, where they attach themselves to the intestinal wall and suck blood. When they detach and move to a new location, the old wound continues to bleed for a while, so bloody diarrhea is often a symptom of hookworms. Hookworm eggs are passed through the feces and are either picked up from stool, as with roundworms, or, if conditions are right, hatch in the soil and attach themselves to the feet of their new host. They burrow through the skin of the feet, then migrate to the intestinal tract where the cycle then repeats itself.

Take care! You can pick up hookworms if you go walking barefoot in infected soil.

The eggs can be detected in a fecal analysis. Treatment often needs to be repeated two or more times before finally ridding the host of the parasites. Good sanitation is necessary to prevent a re-infestation.

Tapeworms

These parasites also live in the intestinal tract, and attach to the wall to absorb nutrients. They grow by creating new segments. Usually the first sign of an infestation is small rice-like segments found around the dog's rectum or in his stool. Tapeworms are acquired when the dog eats an infected flea, the intermediate host. A good flea control program is the best way to prevent tapeworm infestations.

Heartworm

These parasites live in the upper heart and greater pulmonary arteries, where they damage the vessel walls. Poor circulation results, which in turn damages other body functions. Eventually the heart fails and the dog dies.

The adult worms produce thousands of tiny worms, known as microfilaria. These circulate throughout the bloodstream until they are picked up by mosquitoes, the intermediate host. The microfilaria continue to develop in the mosquito. Then, when they're ready, they are transferred to another dog when that mosquito bites the dog.

WORMING OUT THE SECRET

Most internal parasites can be detected by taking a small piece of your dog's stool to the veterinarian's office. The stool will be prepared and then examined under a microscope. Parasites, their eggs, or larvae can then be detected and your vet can prescribe appropriate treatment. After treatment, the vet will ask you to bring in another stool sample – usually in 2 to 3 weeks – to make sure the treatment was effective.

Dogs infested with heartworm can be treated when the infestation is in its early stages. However, heavy infestations are difficult to treat, because the treatment itself is risky. Preventive medications are available, and that is the best way to deal with this problem. They are easy to administer and are very effective. Talk to your veterinarian about heartworm preventives and whether heartworm has been found in your area.

Giardiasis

This is not a worm, but it is a parasite. The protozoa giardia is common in wild animals. If you and your dog go camping or hiking and take a drink from a clear mountain stream, you can both pick up giardia. Diarrhea is one of the first symptoms of this parasite.

If you come home from a camping trip feeling ill, tell your physician and veterinarian you've been in the wild, and have yourself and your dog tested for giardia.

Coccidiosis

This is another parasitic protozoa. This one is often carried by birds. The symptoms include coughing, a runny nose, eye discharge, and diarrhea. It can be diagnosed through a fecal analysis.

■ **Healthy puppies** *are unmistakable. By and large, if your puppy has a healthy-looking coat, is full of energy and vitality, and shows no unusual behavior patterns, you can relax.*

Dangerous diseases

MANY OF THE DISEASES *that threaten your puppy can be prevented with vaccinations. Hopefully, your puppy will be healthy and disease-free and you'll never need to see the diseases listed below. But you should know what to look for, just in case. A detailed description of the common diseases for which vaccination is required, as well as a discussion of vaccination itself, has already been given in Chapter 9 (pp.120-125).*

The main diseases

Consult your vet about vaccinating your puppy for these main infectious diseases, many of which have often proven fatal to dogs in the pre-vaccination days:

- Distemper
- Infectious canine hepatitis
- Coronavirus
- Parvovirus

- Leptospirosis
- Kennel cough
- Bordetella bronchiseptica
- Rabies

Despite vaccination, a puppy may still get sick. Perhaps his immune system is not functioning properly, the organism causing the disease mutated, or the vaccine itself was ineffective.

A simple summary

✔ External parasites, like fleas and ticks, are more than just nuisances. They can transmit disease and endanger your puppy's life.

✔ Internal parasites, like ringworm or hookworm, are nasty and often difficult to get rid of – and some can be transmitted to human beings.

✔ Although vaccinations can prevent many infectious deadly diseases, their effectiveness depends upon the health of your puppy's immune system.

Chapter 14

What to do in an Emergency

Y OU CAN BE THE MOST careful puppy owner in the world and emergencies will still happen. Someone may trip over the puppy, she may fall off the sofa and hit her head, or she may chew on something that makes her sick. It's always scary when your puppy gets hurt, but if you are prepared for emergencies, you will be able to handle them with a little bit less stress.

In this chapter...

✓ Restraining an injured dog

✓ Canine CPR and shock

✓ Heatstroke, bleeding, and choking

✓ Poisons and burns

✓ Gastric torsion (bloat)

✓ Bites and stings

✓ Natural (and other) disasters

173

Restraining an injured dog

YOU MUST KNOW *how to restrain your puppy if she gets hurt, so that she doesn't hurt herself more by struggling, or hurt you when you try to help her. As much as we love our dogs, and as much as they love us, they are still dogs; when a dog is hurt, she doesn't stop to think about how her actions may hurt herself or you. She struggles because she is frightened and in pain. Therefore, you need to know how to restrain her.*

■ **You can make** *a muzzle out of just about anything that is long and soft. A leash works very well, as does a bandanna, or a length of gauze from your first-aid kit.*

Prevent her from biting

You need to learn how to muzzle your pup. By closing her mouth gently but firmly, you can make sure she doesn't bite anyone when she's afraid or hurt. Take the leash or material and wrap it quickly around her snout at least twice. Wrap it gently, not too tight, but firmly. Pull the ends back behind her ears and tie it behind her neck. If you gently pull on the material around the snout, it shouldn't slip off.

Watch your puppy carefully when she's muzzled to make sure she can breathe. If she's having trouble breathing or is getting very anxious, loosen the muzzle slightly.

Canine CPR and shock

CPR (CARDIOPULMONARY RESUSCITATION), *a combination of heart massage and assisted breathing, has saved thousands of people's lives, and can do the same for dogs. If you know CPR you could some day save your dog's life. You should also be aware of the symptoms of shock, which is a life-threatening condition for dogs.*

Call your local Red Cross to find out if they offer classes for pet CPR in your area.

CPR MADE SIMPLE

The best way to offer CPR is with two people: one to do the heart massage and one to do the breathing. But you can do it alone if need be, as shown below. Remember, once you start CPR, continue it until your dog begins breathing on her own, until you can get your dog to help, or until it seems very obvious that it is in vain. But don't stop too soon – many dogs have been saved by canine CPR!

1 Checking for life signs

When you see a dog lying still you need to make a quick evaluation. Check to see if there is a heartbeat. Also check to see if she is breathing.

2 Clearing the mouth

If she's not breathing, clear her mouth of any obstructions. Pull her tongue out and to the side of her mouth so that it doesn't block the airway.

3 Assisted breathing

Inhale a deep breath, and then exhale into the dog's nose. Watch her chest to check that it rises after you blow. Repeat every 10 seconds for big dogs and more often for smaller dogs. After 10 breaths, stop and do chest compressions.

4 Chest compression

Place her on her side and place your hands, one on top of the other, over her heart. Lean over, and push down in short bursts. Compress the chest 5 times, then go back to assisted breathing. Repeat in a cycle of 10 breaths and 5 compressions.

Do not practice CPR on a dog that is not in a life-threatening situation. You could severely hurt her.

Shock is life threatening!

A dog (like a person) can go into *shock* after a traumatic injury or during a serious, sudden illness. By itself, shock is life threatening. When it's combined with whatever caused the shock in the first place, your puppy is in serious danger.

The symptoms

Symptoms of shock include:

1. Faster, often irregular, heartbeat

2. Panting or very rapid breathing, often gasping

3. Dilated pupils, a staring, glazed look to the eyes, and no eye response to movement

Treating shock

All you can do to treat shock is to keep your dog warm and still and get her to a veterinarian right away. This is not the time to watch the dog and hope she'll come out of it on her own. She needs help right away!

<aside>
DEFINITION

Shock is *a life-threatening condition caused by a trauma, that results in insufficient blood flow and oxygen to meet the body's needs. The cardiovascular system of an animal in shock will try to compensate for the lack of oxygen and blood flow by increasing the heart and respiration rates, constricting the blood vessels in the skin and reducing urinary output. This requires additional energy at a time when the vital organs aren't getting enough energy anyway.*
</aside>

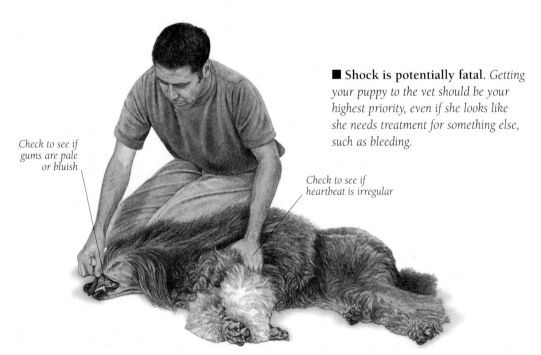

Check to see if gums are pale or bluish

Check to see if heartbeat is irregular

■ **Shock is potentially fatal.** *Getting your puppy to the vet should be your highest priority, even if she looks like she needs treatment for something else, such as bleeding.*

Heatstroke, bleeding, and choking

DOGS LOSE HEAT *by panting, and by sweating through the pads of their feet. Since these are small areas of a dog's body, your puppy can overheat much more quickly than you do. Bleeding injuries are another danger you should look out for, and choking is common among puppies since they love putting things in their mouths.*

■ **Rapid, heavy panting,** *as well as salivation, is a symptom of overheating.*

The number-one cause of heatstroke in dogs is being left alone in cars. Never ever leave a dog shut in a car on a warm day — not even for a moment. A car will heat up to over 100°F in just minutes, even if it's in the 70s outside.

HEATSTROKE AND ITS CURE

A dog that is overheated will lie down, often flopping herself down, or will pace back and forth in agitation. She will pant heavily and may go into shock. Her body temperature will rise rapidly.

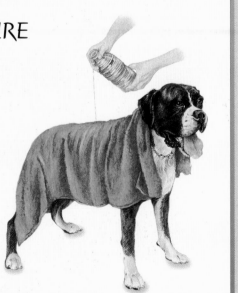

■ **Cool your puppy down** *immediately. Immerse her in cool water or hose her down, cover her with a cold wet towel, and get her to the vet's office right away.*

Bleeding

Bleeding accompanies most kinds of injuries. How it should be treated depends upon the type of bleeding and its severity.

Just a bruise

If the skin isn't broken, there may be bleeding under the skin. This can result in a bruise if the injury is small. A bruise can be treated with an ice pack. Use the ice pack on and off at 15-minute intervals until it seems that the bleeding under the skin has stopped. After 24 hours, use a heat pack to improve blood circulation and healing to the injured site.

KNOW YOUR VET'S EMERGENCY PROCEDURES

Don't wait until there is an emergency to find out what your veterinarian's policies are. Ask now so you know.

1 After hours emergencies

Some vets do not handle after-hours emergencies at all. Instead, they refer their clients to emergency animal hospitals. Other vets take all calls no matter what the hour. There's no right or wrong policy – what's important is that you understand the policy and know who to call when there is an emergency.

2 Local hospital

If your vet refers emergencies to a local animal hospital, do you know where it is? Can you find it right away without having to search for it? If you aren't sure, you should drive around and find it now. Again, don't wait for the emergency to happen. Be prepared.

3 Payment

What are your veterinarian's policies regarding payment for emergency care? What are the policies of the emergency animal hospital? Many require complete payment when they treat your dog. If that's the case, can you pay the bill? Emergency care can be very expensive. What happens if an emergency occurs between paydays?

Post the vet's phone number and the emergency animal hospital's number in several prominent locations – in your wallet, your telephone book, your canine first-aid kit, and on the refrigerator.

If you don't have an ice pack handy in an emergency, use a bag of frozen vegetables. This works just as well.

Scrapes and cuts

Bleeding from small scrapes, scratches, and small cuts is usually not a danger. Wipe it off, and apply pressure with a gauze pad if it's still oozing. When the bleeding stops, rinse it off with hydrogen peroxide. If the wound is red and oozing, rinse it several times a day with hydrogen peroxide and carefully rub an antibiotic ointment on it. If you're concerned, make an appointment to bring your dog in to see the vet. This is not, however, an emergency.

Oozing blood

A continuous, oozing type of bleeding is more serious. Put pressure on the wound, using layers of gauze pads and pressure from your hand, and get the dog to your veterinarian right away. Stitches will probably be required, and if the dog has lost too much blood, additional treatment will be needed.

■ **After an injury,** *continue to check the wound for a few days to make sure it's not infected and is healing well.*

Watch your dog carefully. Too much blood loss can trigger shock and cardiac arrest. Get her to the vet's office right away!

Bleeding in spurts

Bleeding that comes out in spurts is very dangerous. It means a major blood vessel has been broken and your dog is in immediate danger of bleeding to death. Use a length of gauze or a shoelace to make a *tourniquet* about the wound, between the wound and the heart. Wrap the shoelace around her leg, then tie a small stick to the knot. Twist the stick so that it tightens the knot and the shoelace around the leg. You are trying to cut off circulation so that the bleeding slows.

Tourniquets must be loosened every 10 to 15 minutes, or the tissue in the leg will die from lack of blood. You should loosen the tourniquet, let the blood flow for a couple of minutes, and then tighten it again.

> **DEFINITION**
>
> *A* **tourniquet** *is a 'bandage' tied near a bleeding wound in such a way that the blood supply from the heart to the wounded region is cut off.*

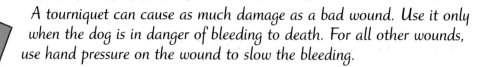

A tourniquet can cause as much damage as a bad wound. Use it only when the dog is in danger of bleeding to death. For all other wounds, use hand pressure on the wound to slow the bleeding.

Internal bleeding

Internal bleeding is less obvious and is very dangerous. If your dog has been in some kind of rough accident, watch her behavior. If she stops moving, acts restless, or cries, get her to the vet's office right away. Other symptoms of internal bleeding include pale gums, a distended abdomen, bloody diarrhea, bloody vomit, or blood in the saliva.

WHAT TO DO FOR CHOKING

Puppies put stuff in their mouths all the time. After all, they don't have hands, and tasting and chewing on things is one of the ways puppies discover their world. Unfortunately, that means puppies (and adult dogs) are in danger of choking. This is what you can do:

1 **Checking**

If your dog seems to be choking, coughing, or gagging, open her mouth and try to see what is blocking her airway.

2 **Removing**

If you can reach it, do so and pull it out. Tongs (such as salad tongs) will help you grasp a round object, such as a ball.

If you can't pull out whatever is in your puppy's throat, try this. Stand above and behind her, reach under her belly just behind the ribcage, and pull up quickly several times. If this doesn't work, don't wait! Her life is at stake — get her to the vet right away.

Poisons and burns

I KNOW YOU PUPPY-PROOFED your house, your yard, and even your garage before you brought home your puppy, and all the dangers you could think of were removed from her reach. Unfortunately, accidents can still happen – more than one puppy has poisoned or burned herself because she was too curious and stuck her nose where it didn't belong.

Telltale signs of poisoning

The symptoms of poisoning can vary depending upon what your puppy ate. The table on p.182 gives a list of some of the more common substances found around the house, and what you should do if your puppy gets into them.

■ **Dogs, especially inquisitive pups,** *are not at all fastidious about what they get into and what they eat.*

Some of the more common poisoning symptoms include extreme salivation and drooling, vomiting, diarrhea, and muscle tremors. The puppy's eyes may be dilated or she may suffer seizures.

What to do

With any case of poisoning, after doing what you can at home, get your puppy to the veterinarian right away. Bring with you whatever it was your puppy got into. If at all possible, bring the label with the name of the product and any ingredients. The more information you can give your vet, the better. A 24-hour poison hotline called National Poison Control Center for Animals is available at (900)-680-0000. No credit card is needed; your phone bill will be charged.

INTERNET

www.doctordog.com/
dogbook/dogch01.html

Doctor Dog's Emergency Section offers illustrated advice on what to do in a variety of emergencies, from burns to electrocution to shock.

EMERGENCY CURES FOR COMMON POISONS

Poison	What you can do
● Antifreeze	Induce vomiting and get your puppy to the vet's office right away
● Bleach	Induce vomiting and take your puppy in to your veterinarian soon, although if she has vomited it is no longer an emergency
● Chocolate	This is poisonous to dogs, so make her vomit and then call your vet
● Gasoline	Make her vomit, give her some vegetable oil to block absorptions, and take her to the vet's office right away
● Ibuprofen	Make her vomit and get her to the vet's office right away
● Insecticides	If ingested, get her to the vet right away. Do not induce vomiting unless your vet recommends it. If there was skin contact, wash her thoroughly, then get her to the vet's right away
● Rodent or roach poison	Induce vomiting and get her to your vet's office right away

You can get your puppy to vomit by giving her several teaspoons of hydrogen peroxide.

Burns

Puppies can get burned in a variety of ways, usually from one of the following categories:

a Thermal burns are caused by heat, and puppies can be burned if they stick their nose on the outside of the charcoal grill after you light it, or investigate a candle, or knock over the iron

b Electrical burns can result from chewing on an electrical cord

c Contact burns can happen from a corrosive substance such as bleach, gasoline, liquid drain cleaner, paint thinner, or road salt

What to do for burns

If you suspect your puppy has been burned, follow these directions:

1 If it's a chemical burn, rinse your puppy thoroughly. Also treat the problem as a potential poisoning

2 For any burn, put an ice pack on the spot

3 If the burn is not severe and the skin is simply red, keep it clean and watch it carefully to make sure it doesn't get infected

4 If the burn has damaged layers of skin, is blistered, bleeding, and oozing, or if the burn has damaged all the layers of skin, cover it lightly and take your puppy to the vet's office right away

Gastric torsion (bloat)

THIS CONDITION IS MORE PREVALENT in large breed dogs with deep chests, such as Great Danes, Rottweilers, German Shepherd Dogs, and Labrador Retrievers. However, it can happen in just about any breed.

What to do

No one is sure what causes bloat, but you can lessen the likelihood by keeping the dog quiet for an hour after each meal, feeding two or three small meals instead of one large meal, and limiting water intake for an hour after each meal.

If you notice your dog has an enlarged abdomen or is pacing, showing extreme restlessness, or gagging without throwing up (especially soon after eating), get her to the vet's office right away. Bloat can be treated if the dog arrives at the vet's office soon enough. Left untreated, it can be fatal!

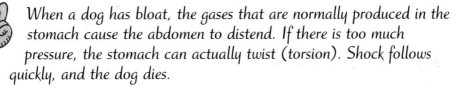

When a dog has bloat, the gases that are normally produced in the stomach cause the abdomen to distend. If there is too much pressure, the stomach can actually twist (torsion). Shock follows quickly, and the dog dies.

Bites and stings

ANY PUPPY THAT SPENDS *some amount of time outside will one day run up against a bug that doesn't want to play with her. Most insect bites and stings are simply an annoyance, and pose no real health threat. However, some dogs are allergic to bee stings, wasp stings, or spider bites. If your dog is allergic, this could be a potentially life-threatening situation.*

■ **Puppies seem to** *search out trouble effortlessly!*

Treating insect bites

If you suspect your dog has been stung or bitten by an insect, first try to find where on your dog's body the bite or sting is. If there is a stinger, scrape it out.

Don't grab an insect stinger and pull – that will squeeze more venom into your dog's skin. Scrape it out with a fingernail.

If you need to, shave away some of the dog's hair so you can see the sting or bite. Wash it off, pour some hydrogen peroxide on it, and watch it.

Allergic reactions

Some signs of allergic reaction include:

● Swelling at the site of the bite or sting, and in the body tissues around it
● Redness or extreme whiteness
● Fever
● Muscle aches, joint pain, and lameness
● Vomiting
● Diarrhea

■ **Hydrogen peroxide** *is useful in many medical emergencies.*

If your puppy is showing any of these allergic reactions, call your veterinarian right away. He or she may recommend that you give your puppy an antihistamine immediately. The vet will also want to see your puppy as soon as you can bring her in.

Wild animal bites

If your dog is bitten by a wild animal, you must get her to the veterinarian's office right away. If your puppy has received her rabies vaccination (usually given between 4 and 6 months of age), that worry will be eliminated. However, if your puppy has not yet received that vaccine, there could be serious consequences. Your vet will also want to treat the wound itself, and may recommend antibiotics.

Wild animals carrying the rabies virus are not uncommon in North America. Skunks, raccoons, bats, and squirrels are all possible carriers. The best prevention is to make sure that your puppy is vaccinated.

Snake bites

Contrary to their reputation, most snakes are not very aggressive. In fact, most of the time you won't see the snakes that are close to you – they will slither away before you know they are near. However, many snakes will defend themselves when threatened, and when your puppy decides to use a snake as a play toy, the snake will consider that a threat! Luckily, the vast majority of snakes are not poisonous (non-venomous).

Dog bites

If your puppy is bitten by another puppy during organized play time and the bite is a simple puncture made with baby puppy teeth, don't be too worried. Simply wash the bite, pour some hydrogen peroxide over it, and watch it. If it looks red and like it may be infected, call your veterinarian.

However, if your puppy is attacked by an unknown dog, call your vet immediately, as this could pose a real health threat. If you can, try to find the dog's owner to make sure the dog is vaccinated, especially with an up-to-date rabies vaccine. Some bites may need special treatment, including antibiotics, draining or stitches, to make sure they heal properly.

■ **Try to regulate** *which dogs your puppy plays with. You don't want her being bitten by an unvaccinated dog.*

A CANINE FIRST-AID KIT

I put together my first canine first-aid kit more than 20 years ago, and am always glad I did. It has been used for a few big emergencies, and numerous small ones. I used it to take care of my dogs, cats, and reptiles, as well as friends' and neighbors' dogs. It has come in handy more times than I can count. I use a large fishing tackle box to hold all my first-aid supplies, because it is big and has a lot of little sections to hold small items. What should you keep in your canine first-aid kit?

Essential supplies

Some of the very basics of a canine first-aid kit are shown below.

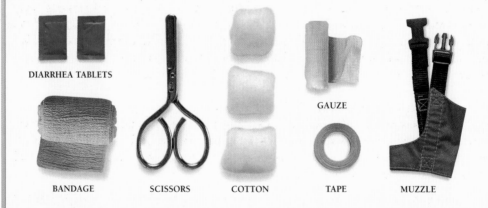

DIARRHEA TABLETS

GAUZE

BANDAGE   SCISSORS   COTTON   TAPE   MUZZLE

Other important items

You should also keep the following items for a canine crisis of the medical kind:

- Large and small tweezers
- Disposable razors
- Nail clippers for dogs
- Thermometer
- Safety pins
- Clean fabric of different widths
- Instant cold compresses
- Elastic to wrap around bandages
- Antiseptic cleansing wipes
- Sterile saline eye wash
- Alcohol prep pads
- Small bottle of hydrogen peroxide
- Antihistamine tablets (such as Benadryl)
- Antiseptic anesthetic spray (such as Bactine)
- Bacitracin antibiotic ointment
- Spare leash and collar
- Mirror
- Pen, pencil, and paper

Natural (and other) disasters

WHERE DO YOU LIVE? *In Southern California where I live, we must deal with wildfires and earthquakes. In the Midwest, dog owners must put up with tornadoes. Families in the Southeast must be able to survive hurricanes. Natural disasters are a fact of life, and you need to make preparations so that you can take care of your puppy as well as your family.*

Keep some supplies on hand

When on a trip, my first-aid kit is in my van. I also have on hand a gallon jug of water – more if we're traveling in the desert. Extra leashes and collars are always in my van, too. My dogs always wear a collar tag with my name and phone number on it, as well as their license tag. They are also tattooed and microchipped for identification.

■ **Keep your first-aid kit,** *whether human or canine, easily accessible!*

A few of my neighbors think I'm a little neurotic, but my husband and I have lived in this area for many years and have been evacuated twice due to wildfires. When you're ordered to evacuate, you don't have any time to pack up. You grab what you can and leave. My emergency kit has come in handy both times we had to leave in a hurry, and it's there for any future emergencies.

A simple summary

✔ Know what your veterinarian's emergency procedures are before there's an emergency. Make sure you know where the emergency animal hospital is located, too.

✔ Practice restraining and muzzling your puppy before an emergency. Make a game out of it for your puppy, but know how to do it.

✔ Put together a first-aid kit, and keep it stocked and handy.

✔ Familiarize yourself with first-aid for a host of canine emergencies, so you'll know what to do.

✔ In any emergency, after you administer aid, take your puppy to the veterinarian immediately.

TOGETHER YOU WILL FIND YOUR WAY

Chapter 15

How to Be Your Puppy's Teacher

YOUR PUPPY WASN'T BORN knowing how to be good, or even wanting to be good for you; he must learn that, and it's your job to teach him. Training is a process that involves both you and your puppy. It should ideally be as positive as you can make it – as positive as your puppy will allow you to make it. When you can set your puppy up for success and prevent as many problems as possible from happening, you and the puppy will both enjoy your life together much more.

In this chapter...

✓ Learning how to teach your puppy

✓ Your voice is a training tool

✓ Your other training tools

✓ You must be your puppy's leader

✓ Make your training successful

How to teach your puppy – simply but surely

YOUR PUPPY WAS BORN *understanding canine communication. He understands canine body language, facial expressions, and verbalizations. Living with people, he must translate everything he sees and hears into this canine language, much the way you'd have to if you were dropped into a totally foreign civilization.*

Communicating requires some effort

To make teaching easier, you want to communicate with him so there is as little misunderstanding as possible. But that's hard, because while your puppy has a hard time understanding you, you understand him even less. It is impossible for people to think like dogs – we just can't do it. We can try, and we can make some relatively educated guesses, but we are always thinking like people, and that affects everything we do with our dogs.

■ **Praise is important** *as a communication tool. When you pat and praise your puppy for relieving himself in the correct spot, you communicate to him that this is where he must relieve himself next time.*

However, we can try to communicate as simply as possible, and that's our goal. If your puppy understands you, then what you're doing is working.

Every time you interact with your puppy you teach him something, and it may (or may not) be what you want him to know! Think about it: What are you teaching him right now?

Your voice is a training tool

YOUR VOICE IS YOUR MOST IMPORTANT training tool. With all my dogs, my ultimate goal is to teach my puppy to listen to my voice, to pay attention, and to respond to verbal commands.

Off leash or on

Once my dog is trained, I want him to respond to my voice when he's off leash. For example, if he is playing out in a field, sniffing and chasing rabbits, I want to be able to call him back to me; I want him to listen to that command and to respond to it right away with no hesitation at all.

I also want him to listen to me around the house, in the car, and in the backyard. I want him to understand that I don't just jabber on for no reason, and that he should pay attention to me when I talk to him.

Your dog should learn to respond immediately to your voice, not only for your day-to-day convenience, but also because it can stop him from getting into trouble in traffic or with other aggressive animals.

■ **After a while,** *your voice is adequate to train your puppy, without the use of other tools such as a leash or treats. It can be used to give a command as well as to praise – both essential parts of training.*

Learning to speak like mom

To make it easier for your puppy to understand, you will be imitating some of the mother dog's verbalizations – or at least her tone of voice. When your puppy was still with his mom, he would interact with her and his littermates using sounds as well as body language. If he wanted to play, his bark was higher in pitch. If a littermate or his mom responded to his play invitation, their barks were also higher in pitch. So we can make a safe assumption that play invitations are higher in pitch than the normal speaking voice, and we can use that to our advantage.

When praising your puppy, say "good boy!" in the tone of voice you used to say "ice cream!" when you were a child. This should be higher in tone than your normal speaking voice, but not as high pitched as a yelp, which might suggest you are hurt.

Trivia...

Mother dogs start training their puppies as soon as possible, and so can you. Your puppy is never too young to learn. In fact, many dog training schools offer puppy kindergarten classes specially geared to a puppy's short attention span and extra energy. They're a good way to get your pup started, and to make sure he is well socialized around other dogs.

Doggy corrections

When your puppy was corrected by his mom – for example, if he bit her with his needle-sharp baby teeth – she would growl at him. That deep growl meant, "You made a mistake! Don't do it again." We can use this sound, too, to our advantage. When your puppy makes a mistake, you can use a deep voice to make a sound such as "Acckk!"

■ **Your puppy's mother** *has already opened the door for you to train him by teaching him with her voice and teeth. She taught him good canine behavior by growling, nipping, or pinning him to the ground.*

It's traditional to correct a dog using the word "no," but this can get confusing. "No" what? Are you saying no to the kids or to the puppy? Are you answering a question or making a correction?

Use a sound that will apply only to the dog and no one else – a sound such as "Acckk!" Then you can teach your puppy a specific vocabulary that includes the word no in a clear context, such as "No bark!" or "No bite!"

Don't correct your puppy with a deep voice and then giggle. You will lose all authority.

No need to scream

If you are normally soft spoken and are concerned about using your voice to control your puppy, don't worry. Use your normal speaking volume, but vary the tones. You are teaching your puppy to listen to you, and if you are naturally soft spoken, that's fine. Your puppy can hear you very well. In fact, it's much better if you never scream at your puppy at all.

THE AGONY OF NEGATIVE ATTENTION

Some dogs, just like some children, will actually work for corrections. These confused souls have discovered that they get attention when they misbehave, and are willing to put up with the yelling, collar corrections, and other negative attention because after all, it is attention.

Usually a puppy like this has some problem behaviors and is often in trouble. His owners yell at him more than anything else, so the puppy soon equates yelling with owner attention. (Remember, to dogs, attention is anything you do that has them as the focus, whether it's negative or positive.) He continues to get into trouble just so he can get attention – any attention, even negative attention. To change this scenario:

1. Focus on giving the puppy attention for good behavior

2. Ignore bad behavior and do not correct it. Remember, correction is attention

3. When the negative attention decreases and the good behavior is rewarded, the dog's focus will change

Striking a balance between praise and correction

Dogs do not learn what to do by being corrected. A correction can let your puppy know when he has made a mistake, but it cannot tell him what to do instead. Praise and positive reinforcements are what let your puppy know when he did something right.

If your puppy is jumping up on you, you can tell him "Acckk! No jump!" as he leaps up. But that alone is not enough to stop the problem. If you follow that up by shaping him into a sit and telling him, "Good boy to sit!" and pet him while he's sitting, he learns an acceptable alternative.

Look at it this way. He's jumping on you for attention, so:

1. Correct the jumping when he leaps up

2. Show him a better way: Have him sit in front of you

3. Praise and pet him for sitting

Don't spare the praise

Much of your puppy's training can be approached in this manner. Let him know when he's made a mistake, and then show him what he can do instead. Show him the right way and praise him enthusiastically for doing it.

When your dog is doing something right, always praise him. If he's lying on the floor quietly chewing on his toy (and not chewing on your nearby shoes) praise him for chewing on his toy.

All good dog training rewards desired actions or behaviors and discourages or ignores undesired actions.

■ **Persistent jumping** *is a problem among puppies who get used to being carried around or sitting in the lap of their owners.*

Other training tools for your puppy

TRAINING TOOLS HELP YOU *teach your puppy to pay attention to you and listen to what you have to say. If your puppy had been born understanding human language and full of the desire to do what you tell him, you wouldn't need training tools. However, your puppy needs to be motivated to do what you ask him. That's why you need training tools.*

Buckle collar

A simple collar with a buckle can be made of leather or nylon. It holds your puppy's identification tags. In training, it is used to connect the leash to your puppy and will restrain him, and that's about it.

■ **A buckle collar's** *main use as a training tool is to restrain your puppy.*

Training collar

This collar is also sometimes called a slip chain collar or a choke chain. It works with a snap and release motion – you snap up and release down. It can be a very effective training collar when used properly. However, when used improperly it can choke the dog. Never jerk this collar hard and never hold it tight. Don't allow you puppy to pull it tight either, because it can choke him.

TRAINING COLLAR

A training collar should never be left on a dog when he isn't supervised.

When you use this collar to give a correction, always use your voice as well. "Acckk! No pull!"– snap and release. Otherwise your puppy may think the snap is simply a movement and has no meaning.

■ **A training collar** *tightens around the dog's neck when you tug at the leash.*

Prong or pinch collar

A prong or pinch collar doesn't choke the dog, but instead gives a pinching correction. This collar look like a medieval torture device, but it can be an effective training tool for some dogs. This collar also works with a snap and release, but a snap with much less force than the slip or training collar. Again, always use your voice when you use this collar to give a correction.

Pinch or prong collars are not the best choice for young puppies.

Head halters

Head halters follow the principle "Where the head goes, the body will follow." They do not choke the dog, nor do they give a hard correction. Instead, the dog is guided to do the right thing. As with the collars, always use your voice to teach the dog that you want him to wear the head halter.

■ **A head halter** *may look like a muzzle but, in fact, it's more like a horse's halter. Your puppy can even drink water when he's wearing it.*

Leash

A leash attaches to the collar or halter so that you have a way to use the collar or halter to teach the puppy. A collar alone won't do much – you must be able to use it, and that's where the leash comes in.

If your puppy likes to chew on his leash, dip it in vinegar before hooking it up to his collar. He'll take one bite and spit it out.

■ **Your puppy may chew** *on his leash, or take it in his mouth, but this is a habit you should not encourage. You're the boss, and you hold the leash.*

Motivators and positive reinforcements

These are things your puppy likes that you will use to motivate him to learn. They can be food treats, squeaky toys, furry toys, or even a tennis ball. They can be used to help your puppy do what you want (as a lure, for example), or can be a reward for doing something right.

To keep a motivator special, give it to your puppy only when you are working with him. Never give it to him for no reason.

Biscuit

■ **Let your puppy know** *that you have a treat at hand when you begin training. It'll teach him the connection between doing what you want and getting a treat.*

Using your training tools

These tools, no matter what they are, should be used as much as possible. If you use the training tools only during training sessions, your puppy will think the behavior he is learning during those sessions is only for use then. If you use the training tools often during your daily routine, your puppy will understand that good behavior is part of his daily routine.

Here are some examples of how to use one of the simplest of your training tools – the leash:

(a) The leash can be used as an umbilical cord to your puppy. If he decides to sneak away from you to a back room where he might get into trouble, use the leash to keep him with you

(b) If your puppy likes to play keep-away, dashing back and forth but never letting you touch him, simply step on the end of the leash and stop the game

(c) If your puppy likes to steal things that belong to you or to other members of the family, use the leash to stop him from running away with the stolen item

I will give you additional examples of how to use your training tools around the house and yard as we go along.

INTERNET

www. legacy-by-mail.com

For clickers, whistles, and training treats, as well as collars, leashes, training books, videos, and tips from top trainer Terry Ryan, check out Legacy's on-line catalog.

Putting it all together

When you teach your puppy, you will use your training tools. Although it may seem right now that there is a lot to remember about these tools, it isn't that difficult. Once you get some practice, it will become second nature to you. You have the following tools:

- A collar or head halter
- A leash, either regular length or long length
- Motivators and positive reinforcements
- Your voice

In the next few chapters, as I show you how to teach the individual exercises, I will also show you how to use your training tools for each command or exercise. Right now just make sure you are comfortable with your training tools.

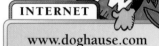

INTERNET

www.doghause.com

This fun site has dog cartoons, quotes, stories, and more.

You must be your pup's leader

YOU ARE NOT YOUR PUPPY'S BEST FRIEND – *at least not yet – nor should you try to be. Instead, you must be your puppy's leader. If he were living with other dogs instead of people, an older dog would assume the leadership position. This dog would demand certain behaviors or actions from subordinates, and your puppy would be one of the subordinates.*

Naturally, you are not a dog and your puppy is not living in a dog pack. But he is comfortable with the canine pack structure and will feel safer and more secure if you are the leader.

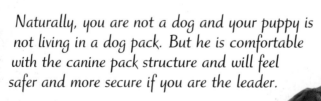

■ **Puppies** *instinctively recognize a leader. This is a legacy from canine pack behavior where the "top dog" would lead by virtue of his strength, intelligence, and willpower.*

What a puppy wants from a leader

The leader, according to your puppy, is the biggest, strongest, fastest, and smartest. Now, not all leaders actually are those things, but if they aren't, they act like they are. Many small dogs are the leaders of much bigger dogs. What they lack in size they make up for in attitude. So act like the leader! The leader is confident. If you are not yet confident about training, at least act like you are!

a The leader of the pack always eats first and best. You should always eat first, even if it's just an apple

b The leader always goes first. Don't let the puppy dash through doorways ahead of you. Don't allow him to dash out of the house or into the house ahead of you

■ **Make your puppy wait** *at all doorways, car doors, and the garden gate.*

c The leader establishes the rules. It's your house, you pay the bills, and you have every right to set some rules

*You **MUST** assume the leadership position! If you don't, your puppy will take on that role as he grows up. If he does, you are going to be in big trouble.*

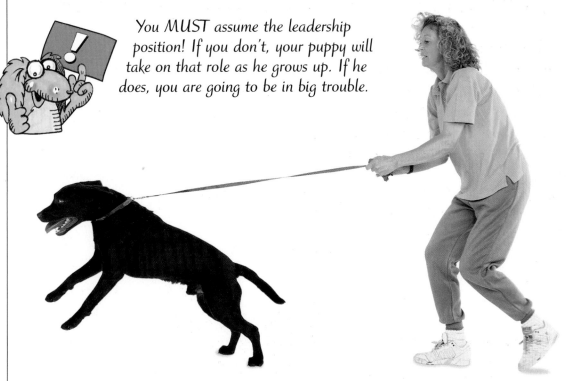

■ **A dog who doesn't feel** *that you are his leader will try to be in charge of you instead. Such dogs are often very confused about their role in the household. They become highly aggressive and dominating.*

Ten simple principles for successful training

THERE ARE SOME BASIC PRINCIPLES *that apply to all dog training. Following them will help make your training more successful.*

1. Show your puppy exactly what to do, help him do it, and praise him when he does it correctly

2. Always give only one command. Do not repeat the word over and over and over again. If you repeat it, which one counts? Which one should he respond to?

3. Consistency is important. Once you establish some rules – such as keeping the puppy off the furniture – you must consistently enforce them

4. Timing is critical to your training success. Praise your puppy as he is doing something right. Correct your puppy as he makes a mistake. Praise and corrections that happen later are not effective

5. Correction (any correction, including voice, collar, or any other training tools) should be forceful enough to stop unwanted behavior, and that's all. Excessive corrections or punishment after the fact will not teach the puppy effectively, and could easily cause him to shy away from you or avoid you

6. You don't need to yell, scream, or shout at your puppy. A loud, frightening voice will not stop unwanted behavior and will threaten your relationship with him

7. You do have to mean what you say. If you correct the puppy and then giggle or laugh when he makes a mistake, your puppy will not take you seriously. Believe in what you are doing

8. Keep in mind that bad behavior is not directed at you personally. Your puppy is not chewing on the sofa and thinking, "Ha! I'll chew this up and that will teach him to go off to work and leave me alone!"

9. Never train your puppy when you are drunk or under the influence of drugs. Don't train your puppy when you're angry

10. Don't train your puppy when the pressures of the day will cause you to take out your frustrations on him

The final commandment: Always end on a high note

Always finish a training session with a success. Stop when your dog has successfully learned something or when he does something very well. You and he will both finish the session feeling good.

You must be patient. It will take time for your puppy to learn new things and even more time for him to figure out that these new things are important to you.

If your puppy is having a hard time with a particular lesson, ask him to do something you know he can do well. After he does it, stop the training session there. You can then still end on a high note.

■ **When praising** *your pup, pat him along his body. A pat on the head is more a gesture of dominance than of praise.*

A simple summary

✔ Your voice, the leash and collar, and the things you use to motivate your dog, such as treats or toys, are your training tools.

✔ Training tools should be used all the time, in day-to-day practical situations, and not just during training sessions.

✔ You must be your puppy's leader. It's natural and he expects it.

✔ Set up your training to give your pup every opportunity to succeed.

✔ Always end your training session with something you know your puppy can do well.

Chapter 16

Basic Training

EIGHT BASIC OBEDIENCE COMMANDS should be a part of every dog's vocabulary. Just as different children learn in different ways, so do different puppies. I'll explain more than one way to teach each of these commands and I'm sure you'll find one that will work for your puppy.

In this chapter...

✓ Let's start with the basics

✓ Teaching "sit" and "release"

✓ Teaching "lie down"

✓ Teaching "stay"

✓ Teaching your pup "come"

✓ Teaching "watch me," "let's go," and "heel"

✓ Tips for top training sessions

YOU WON'T BE A VICTIM OF ROAD RAGE IF YOU TRAIN YOUR PUPPY WELL

Let's start with the basics

THE EIGHT BASIC COMMANDS are "sit," release, "lie down," "stay," "come," "watch me," "let's go," and "heel." These commands teach your puppy several skills, all of which are important for her behavior at home and out in public. Some of the commands teach your puppy to control herself – to be aware that there are consequences to her actions. She will learn that if she controls herself, does what you ask of her, and restrains her desires to run and jump and play (at least for the moment), she will be praised. If she doesn't restrain herself, there will be no praise and there might be a **correction**.

> **DEFINITION**
>
> A **correction** is a verbal or physical way of telling the dog she's made a mistake. The correction should always be as mild as you can make it while still getting your point across.

Skills to prevent problems

In other situations, a command may serve as an alternative behavior to prevent problems. For example, your puppy cannot jump on people if she learns to sit for praise and petting. She cannot drag you down the street if she learns to walk nicely on the leash while watching you.

Any training you decide to do later with your puppy rests on the eight basic commands. She'll need to understand them thoroughly before she can go on to any advanced training or any dog sports or activities.

■ **A well-trained puppy** *will be obedient, comfortable among new people and situations, and less likely to exhibit canine bad behavior.*

Teaching "sit" and release

TEACHING YOUR PUPPY TO SIT *is relatively easy. Teaching her to sit still is harder, but we'll take this in small steps and set her up to succeed. We'll also teach her the command to release her from sitting. I'll pretend your dog's name is Sweetie (she is one, isn't she?), but you can just fill in your dog's name.*

What "sit" means

You want your puppy to understand that the word "sit" means "Put your hips on the ground, keeping your front end up, and be still." Obviously, you cannot tell your puppy this and expect her to understand, so your must teach her that's what it means. I have found two methods for teaching "sit" very effective.

A SIMPLE WAY TO TEACH "SIT"

This method is based upon using a treat to lure your puppy into sitting.

1 **Show a treat**

With your puppy on her leash close to you, show her a treat. Keep it above her head so she has to reach up to sniff it.

2 **Bring it overhead**

Move it over her head and back toward her tail as you say, "Sweetie, sit." When her head follows the treat, her hips will automatically go down.

3 **Give praise**

Remember to actually give her the treat and praise her enthusiastically when she sits. This will reinforce the "sit" command.

ANOTHER WAY TO TEACH "SIT"

If you use a treat, your puppy may spin around trying to get the treat, rather than sitting. In that case, put the treat away in your pocket and try this method of physically shaping her into a sitting position.

1 Hand on chest

Put one hand on your puppy's chest where the chest and neck meet.

2 Push backwards

Tell her "Sweetie, sit," and at the same time, push that hand slightly up and back (thereby pushing her chest up and back).

3 Slide downwards

Simultaneously, let the other hand slide down her back toward the hips and tuck her hips down and under.

■ **Think of a teeter-totter** *when making your puppy sit: move her up and back at the chest and down and under at the hips.*

Praise and correction

You can teach your puppy what sitting means by using your voice. When she does sit, praise her in a higher-than-normal tone of voice, "Good girl to sit!" When she begins to move from position – not after she's gone, but right when she starts to move – use your growling tone of voice, "Acckk!" and put her back in the sit position.

Keep in mind that most dog breeds were developed to do a job of some kind. As a pet, this job is missed. Sitting for everything she wants can be your puppy's first job!

How useful is "sit"?

"Sit" is a very useful command, not just as the foundation for more advanced commands, but also for everyday use around the house.

● Have her sit when you fix her dinner. She can't jump on you and knock the bowl out of your hands when she's sitting

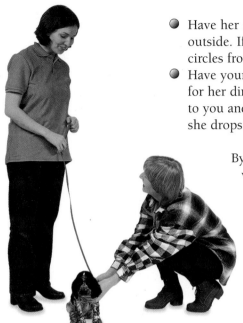

- Have her sit when you hook up her leash to take her outside. If she's sitting, she can't be spinning around in circles from excitement
- Have your puppy sit for everything she wants: for petting, for her dinner, for treats, and for toys. When she comes up to you and nudges you to pet her, have her sit first. When she drops her tennis ball at your feet, have her sit first

By teaching your puppy to sit for everything she wants, you are setting up some rules for her behavior and giving her structure (which is important to a young puppy). Equally important, you are giving her a job to do.

■ **Have your puppy sit** *to be petted by visitors, especially if she likes to jump on people. She can't jump up and sit at the same time.*

Two ways to teach the release

Once your puppy is sitting, what do you do next? Do you just let the puppy get up? How does she know when she's done with the "sit"? The release command "OK!" means, "You're done now, you can move." With this command, the puppy knows exactly when she's allowed to move from position. This can be taught in two ways:

1. With your puppy sitting, pat her on the shoulder as you tell her "OK!" in a high-pitched tone of voice, and encourage her to get up from the "sit" by raising your hands high. If you lift your hands up and bounce a little yourself, she will probably bounce up, too, copying your movements

2. With your puppy sitting, pat her on the shoulder as you tell her "OK!" in a high-pitched tone of voice. Use the leash to gently move her from the "sit"

Using the release

The primary purpose of the release command is to alleviate confusion: The puppy knows exactly when she's done.

Use both a touch and a verbal command for releasing your puppy from the sitting position. If you use only a word, the puppy could release herself whenever she hears the release command used in ordinary conversation.

Teaching "lie down"

TEACHING YOUR PUPPY to lie down can be easy, but just as with the "sit," lying down and being still can be a little harder! I use the phrase "lie down" because "down" by itself is used for so many other things. If you tell your puppy "down" when she jumps on you and "down" when you want her to get off the furniture, which meaning should she respond to? And neither of those uses is exactly the same as "lie down." Each command must have only one meaning. You can't expect a puppy to understand the nuances of context.

A handy tip

Both the methods described here need you to physically impel your puppy to lie down. Take care that you don't let her turn this into a wrestling contest. If she starts to thrash around, use your voice, "Acckk!" and your hands to make her lie down. If she continues to thrash, use your voice again and the leash to give her a snap-and-release correction.

A SIMPLE WAY TO TEACH "LIE DOWN"

In this method you have to use a treat as a lure and slight pressure from your hand. However, don't push! If you push, your puppy may simply push back. When she's down, give her the treat and praise her.

1 **Show a treat**

Have your puppy sit. With a treat in one hand and another hand on the puppy's shoulder, tell her, "Sweetie, lie down," as you let her sniff the treat.

2 **Help to lie down**

Move the treat to the ground in front of her forepaws (lead her nose down with the treat). Assist her in this downward movement with the hand on her shoulder.

"Lie down" can be a handy command

The "lie down" command is a very useful and handy command, both at home and out in public places. You can use it in conjunction with the "stay" command, which I'll be teaching you next.

- Have the puppy lie down during meals so that she isn't begging under the table. Place her where you can see her, but away from the table
- Have her lie down at your feet while talking to guests. She can't be jumping all over them or knocking their drinks over if she's still lying at your feet
- Have her lie down with a toy when you would like to have some quiet time to read
- Have her lie down while you're talking to a neighbor
- Have her lie down while you get your mail out of the box and sort through it

The "lie down" command is a good exercise to help establish your position as leader. Have your puppy lie down at your feet while you are sitting or standing above her. Do this at least once (more is better) every single day.

ANOTHER WAY TO TEACH "LIE DOWN"

In this method you have to scoop your puppy's legs up and out, while assisting her to lie down. Remember to speak the command "lie down" as you do this.

1 **Grasp forelegs**

Reach over your puppy's shoulders with one arm to grasp the front leg away from you, while your other hand grasps the closest leg.

2 **Ease puppy down**

Ease her down gently – you must not hurt her – and help her hold the position for a few seconds. Tell her "Sweetie, lie down."

Teaching "stay"

THE "STAY" COMMAND IS USED with "sit" and "lie down." You want your puppy to understand that "stay" means, "Remain in this position while I walk away, and stay here until I come back to you and release you."

The "sit" and "lie down" commands by themselves teach your pup to hold that position until you release her, but only while you are with her. With "stay," you'll be able to walk away from her.

How long can a puppy stay:

Don't be in a hurry to move away from your puppy or to have her stay for longer time periods. It is very difficult for puppies to hold still, and right now it's important that your puppy succeeds in her training. Here are some reasonable expectations for sit-stays for a young puppy 12 to 16 weeks old:

- **First week of training**: one to two steps away for 10 seconds
- **Second week**: three to four steps away for 10 seconds
- **Third week**: three to four steps away for 15 to 20 seconds
- **Fourth week**: six to eight steps away for 20 seconds

A SIMPLE WAY TO TEACH "STAY"

1 Signal with hand

Have your puppy sit. Hold your open palm in front of her face about 2 inches from her nose. Tell her "Sweetie, stay!"

2 Step away

Take a step or two away. If she moves, use your voice, "Acckk!" and put her back in position. Wait a few seconds and then step back to her.

3 Teach to remain still

Have her remain still while you praise and pet her, then release her with the release command.

■ **You can teach your puppy** to stay using only your hand. There is no need to use either a leash or treats.

After practicing the "stay" with "sit," try it with "lie down." The training methods are the same, except that you begin by telling the puppy to lie down. You should be the one who decides this. If you ask her to "sit-stay" and she decides to lie down, correct her and help her back up into a sit. She doesn't get to choose the exercise, you do.

Many uses for "stay"

Use "stay" around the house in conjunction with "sit" and "lie down." Just look at your house, your routine and where you might be having some problems with your puppy's behavior. Where can the "stay" help you?

- When guests come over, have the puppy lie down by your feet and tell her to stay. Then she cannot be tormenting your guests with demands for attention
- When you want her to stay away from the table while you're eating, have her lie down and tell her to stay
- Tell your puppy to sit and stay while you're fixing her dinner so she doesn't jump up for her dish
- Have her sit and stay at doors, gates, and curbs so you teach her to await permission
- Have her sit when you meet people while taking a walk
- Have her sit while you go to fetch the post

ANOTHER WAY TO TEACH "STAY"

1 Signal with hand

Have your puppy on a leash and tell her to sit. Hold your open palm in front of her nose and tell her "Sweetie, stay!"

2 Step away

In one hand hold the leash up from her neck, without holding it tightly. Take a step away while you continue to hold the leash up.

3 Correct with leash

If she moves, tell her "Acckk!" as you give her a snap and release correction with her leash, and then give her the release command.

■ **Have your puppy lie down** (instead of sitting) and practice "stay" with her using the steps described here. "Lie down-stay" is easier than "sit-stay" for most puppies.

Teaching your pup "come"

"COME" IS A COMMAND that could one day save your puppy's life. When I teach my dogs to come when called, I want them to understand that "come" means, "Stop what you're doing and come to me right now, with no hesitation, as fast as you can run." This instant response might save your dogs from a dangerous situation – perhaps a dog fight, being hit by a car, or a snake in the grass.

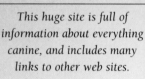

INTERNET

www.dogs.about.com

This huge site is full of information about everything canine, and includes many links to other web sites.

How to teach "come" with a shaker

It's simple to teach your puppy to come to you in gradual stages, with the help of a shaker and some treats.

1 Take a small plastic container, such as a margarine tub, and put a handful of dry kibble dog food in it. Put the top on. If you shake it, you will hear a nice rattling sound. With your puppy sitting in front of you, have the shaker in one hand and some good treats in the other. Shake the shaker and tell your puppy in a happy tone of voice "Cookie!" (or whatever word she knows for treats), and then pop a treat into her mouth

2 You are building a relationship in your puppy's mind between the sound of the shaker and the word "cookie," and between the word "cookie" and the fact that

WHAT IF SHE HESITATES?

If your puppy hesitates about coming to you – especially if something is distracting her – there are some tricks you can use to make her come. First, don't chase her. That will only make her run farther and faster away from you. Instead, call her name in an exciting (not scolding) tone of voice and then run away from her. She will turn and chase after you.

Don't call your puppy to come and do anything she dislikes (take a bath, for example). Make the "come" positive and fun all the time.

she's going to get a treat. Practice this two or three times, and then stop for this training session. You can come back and do it again later in the day

3 After two or three days of this training, stop using "cookie" and say "come," but keep everything else the same. Start with your puppy sitting in front of you. Shake the shaker, say "Sweetie, come!" and pop the treat into her mouth. Now you're changing the equation. The sound of the shaker equals the word "come," which equals the treat popped into her mouth. Practice this for several days, two or three times per session

4 When she's sitting in front of you with her mouth open, waiting for the treat, start backing away from the puppy as you say "Sweetie, come!" Lure her with the treat in front of her nose as you back away. After a few steps, pop the treat into her mouth and praise her, "Good girl to come!"

In a week or two, depending upon how enthused your puppy is, you can stop having her sit in front of you. Instead, when she's across the room from you, pick up the shaker, call her and when she charges across the room to you, praise her and pop the treat into her mouth.

How to teach come with a leash

You can also use a leash to help your puppy avoid distractions when you are teaching her to come.

1 Have your puppy on a leash. Hold the leash in one hand and have some treats in the other

2 Back away from your puppy as you call her, "Sweetie, come!" Make sure you back up a few steps so she gets a chance to chase you

3 If she doesn't come to you right away, use the leash to make sure she does. Praise her when she does come to you, saying "Good girl to come!"

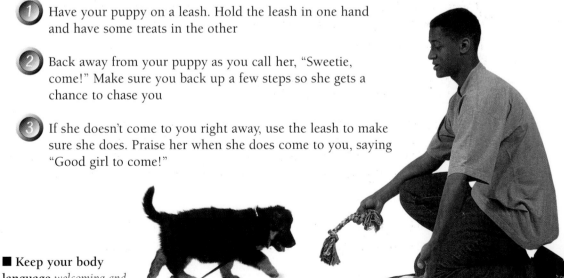

■ **Keep your body language** *welcoming and enthusiastic while training your puppy to come.*

Never correct your puppy for anything to do with learning the command "come." Timing is vitally important, and if she misunderstands a correction, she could learn that coming to you is bad and results in a correction.

Other tricks

As your puppy learns to come and is responding to it well, add some games to the practice. Some other tricks will help your puppy come to you.

1 Lie down on the ground, hide your face, and call her

2 Bend over and scratch at the ground as if you're looking at something very interesting. Ask your puppy, "What's that?" in an "ice cream" tone of voice. When she gets up to you, don't reach out and grab her: You'll never fool her again. Instead, continue to talk to her in an excited tone of voice as you gently take hold of her collar and praise her for coming to you

3 Call her back and forth between two family members and offer her a treat each time she comes

■ **It is important** *that your puppy associates the "come" command with fun and excitement. This will ensure an instant response from her.*

Puppy tails – "come" works

My dogs were in the front yard with me one day as I was washing my car. I heard my older dog growl, so I looked up. The dog down the street, who is known for being quite aggressive with other dogs, was heading our way. I told my older dogs to stay, but as I reached for my puppy, she was already heading toward the aggressive dog! I called her, "Kes, come!" As I got ready to chase after her, I realized she had already stopped, turned around, and was heading back to me. The training worked!

Teaching "watch me," "let's go," and "heel"

TRAINING YOUR PUPPY can be very difficult if you can't get her to pay attention to you. Most pups will focus on their owner at home, but when out in public, the puppy wants to pay attention to everything else. You can help your puppy succeed by teaching her how to pay attention with the "watch me" command, develop her on-leash skills with the "let's go" command, and help her keep close to you in public with "heel."

A SIMPLE WAY TO TEACH "WATCH ME"

When you tell your pup "watch me," you want her to look at your face, preferably at your eyes. She should ignore any distractions and focus on you. In the beginning, this focus may only last a few seconds. But later, as she gets better at it and as her concentration improves, she should be able to focus on you and ignore distractions for minutes at a time.

1 **Show a treat**

Have some treats and have your puppy sitting in front of you and with treats in one hand. First let the puppy sniff the treat so she knows you have it.

2 **Lure with treat**

Say, "Sweetie, watch me!" and at the same time move the treat she was sniffing up to your chin. This movement and position are important.

■ **If your puppy gets distracted** *and looks away, don't lose patience. Use the treat to get her attention back on you.*

215

Another way to teach "watch me"

This method makes use of a training leash to teach your puppy.

1 Show a treat

With your puppy on a leash sitting in front of you, hold the leash in one hand and treats in the other. Say "watch me" and bring the treat to your chin simultaneously.

2 Snap the leash

If the puppy gets distracted or looks away, use a quick snap and release of the leash and collar to let the puppy know she's not to look away. Snap and release – "Acckk! Watch me!"

3 Praise

As soon as she acknowledges the correction and looks back to you, praise her, "Good girl to watch me!"

■ **A leash combined with treats** *is a good "carrot and stick" method of training. However, the leash should only be snapped to take the pup's mind away from distractions, not to punish her.*

Make "watch me" challenging

As your puppy learns the "watch me" command, you can start making her training more challenging.

1. Tell your puppy, "Sweetie, watch me!" and then back away so that she has to watch you while walking

2. When she can follow you for a few steps, back away in a zigzag pattern

3. Back away quickly, then slowly

Of course, when the puppy can do this and has fun following you, you should praise her enthusiastically.

Two ways to teach "let's go"

Good on-leash skills are necessary for all dogs and the "let's go" command will help teach those skills. There are, again, two methods to teach this command: Your goal with either method is to keep the leash slack as your puppy follows you, paying attention to your every move. And of course, when she does, you will praise her enthusiastically!

1 Have your puppy on the leash, and hold the end in one hand. Show her a treat, tell her, "Sweetie, let's go" and simply back away from her. If she watches you, praise her. If she follows you, praise her even more. If she sniffs the ground, looks away from you, or tries to pull in the other direction, use a snap and release of the leash and a verbal correction, "Acckk! No pull!" (or "No sniff!" if that's appropriate). After the correction, if she looks back up to you, praise her

■ **Your aim is to keep** *the leash slack. Don't let your puppy fight or pull on it.*

2 With your puppy on the leash and the leash held securely, walk forward as you tell her, "Sweetie, let's go!" If your puppy dashes past you to pull forward, simply make an about-turn so that you are going in the opposite direction. Without saying anything to your puppy, just hold the leash securely, turn and go. Your puppy will hit the end of the leash as you turn, and when she does, act surprised, "Wow! What happened?" When she turns to go with you, praise her. However, if she dashes past you again, turn around again, repeating the entire exercise

Back away from your puppy several times in different directions. Every time she pulls away, sniffs at something, or ignores you, correct her.

■ **While teaching "let's go,"** *you may have to go back and forth a few times. However, your puppy will soon understand that it's to her advantage to pay attention and walk where you walk.*

Teaching "heel"

The command "heel" means, "Walk by my left side with your neck and shoulder area next to my left leg, maintaining that position no matter what I do." With that definition, if you walk fast, jog, walk slowly, or simply amble, your puppy should maintain the heel position. If you have to walk through a crowd and zigzag around people, your dog should still maintain that position.

Since learning "heel" requires a great deal of concentration on your puppy's part, don't start teaching "heel" until your puppy has been doing the "watch me" command for several weeks (not days – weeks!) and has been doing "let's go" very well for at least 2 weeks, with regular practice.

A SIMPLE WAY TO TEACH "HEEL"

This training is like a little walking session. Keep each session short, enthusiastic, and fun. Once your puppy starts walking to heel, make it challenging by turning, walking fast, walking slowly, and going in different directions.

1 **Back away**

With your puppy on a leash, hold the leash in your left hand and some treats in the right. Back away from your puppy as you say "let's go."

2 **Turn around**

Let her catch up with you as you back up slightly, and turn so that you are facing the same direction she is, so that she ends up on your left side.

3 **Say "heel"**

Walk forward together as you show her a treat and tell her, "Sweetie, heel!" Stop after a few steps, and praise her as you give her the treat.

Keep it interesting

When you take your puppy for a walk, don't ask her to heel the entire way. Instead, go back and forth between "let's go" and the two different methods of teaching "heel." Offer some variety and some challenge.

Once you start training your puppy to "heel," don't let her pull on the leash — ever! Whenever she is on leash, she is to respect it and never, ever pull on it.

ANOTHER WAY TO TEACH "HEEL"

This method requires a little more concentration, so make sure you keep the sessions short and upbeat, and praise the puppy's successes.

1 Say "watch me"

Have your puppy sit by your left side, on a leash, and hold the leash in your left hand. Have some treats in your right hand. Show the puppy a treat and tell her, "Sweetie, watch me!"

2 Give correction

When she's paying attention to you, tell her, "Sweetie, heel!" and walk forward. If she pulls ahead, use the leash to give her a snap and release correction as you tell her, "Acckk! No pull!"

3 Give praise

When she slows down, backs off the pulling and looks back to you, praise her and repeat the "watch me" command. When she watches you, praise her enthusiastically.

■ **If your puppy is alert and eager** *to do the things you are training her to do, her body language will be positive – she will move her body upward and forward.*

A simple training session

When my dog Kes was a puppy, a training session might have gone like this:

1. We'd start with several "sits" and "watch me's," so I'd make sure I had all her attention

2. We'd practice the "let's go" with some back-aways, some turns, and some fast-paced walking

3. We'd do a few quick, short "heel" sessions, and then I'd release her and praise her

4. I'd toss her tennis ball a few times and call her to "come" to me as she brought it back

5. I'd then have her do a "sit-stay," followed by a "down-stay"

6. I'd do another quick "heel," and then we'd be through for this training session

Tips for top training sessions

KEEP YOUR TRAINING SESSIONS FUN. Make sure your puppy learns what she needs to learn, and don't allow her to ignore you. This way, you can enforce your leadership position and still have fun training.

Fun and practice

Every training session will be different, but in all of them I try to keep the training upbeat yet enforced. I want my dogs to want to be good and to want to do these things for me, so I keep it fun. But I also want them to take it seriously. Training is not a game, so I always enforce my rules.

It's important to practice the basic commands in the house, in the yard, in the car, and out in public. Make sure your pup understands these commands are in effect all the time – not just during her training sessions.

A simple summary

✔ The basic commands are the foundation for everything you will ever teach your puppy in the future.

✔ There is more than one way to teach your puppy, and no one technique is right for every dog. Try the different methods I've explained and use the one that is more effective with your dog. Or use them both.

✔ The eight basic commands – "sit," release, "lie down," "stay," "come," "watch me," "let's go," and "heel" – have many useful applications at home and outside.

✔ Keep your training sessions fun and upbeat but under control.

✔ Use these commands everywhere and in all places, not just during training sessions.

Chapter 17

There's More You Can Teach

AFTER THE 8 BASIC COMMANDS, I'll now explain how to teach the next level of commands. With each level of training, you gain more control over your puppy while he learns more self-restraint. Remember, there's no limit to the dog sports, activities, and games you can play together, as you explore your puppy's capacity to learn.

In this chapter...

✓ Teaching "wait"

✓ Teaching respect for boundaries

✓ There's more you can do with "come"

✓ Teaching "stand"

✓ Teaching "go to bed"

✓ Teaching "leave it"

THERE'S NO END TO WHAT SOME DOGS CAN LEARN!

Teaching "wait"

WHEN YOU TAUGHT YOUR PUPPY to "stay," you made him understand that stay means, "Hold this position until I come back to you to release you." However, in some situations it may not be easy for you to go back to release him (remember, the release is done with a touch as well as a verbal command). You may want to take the trash out through the gate, so you'll give the "sit" command. But when you have taken the trash out, you're going to get in your car and leave for work. If you told him to stay, you should really go back to him to release him, right? You don't expect him to do a "sit-stay" in the yard all day!

Using "wait" as a temporary "stay"

The "wait" command is a temporary hold. You want the dog to understand that "wait" means, "Hold this position as I walk away from you, but pay attention because another command is going to follow." The other command will be given at a distance. With the trash and the front gate, you'd do it this way: Have your puppy sit, tell him "wait," open the gate, take the garbage cans out (closing the gate behind you), and then tell your puppy, "Dax, OK" from outside the gate.

The words "wait" and "stay" sound very alike, but your puppy's hearing is very good. Speak clearly when teaching him, and he'll quickly learn the difference between the two words.

Using "wait" in real life

Look at your daily routine. In which practical situations can you use the "wait" command?

- Have your puppy wait before you give him permission to jump into or out of the car
- Have him wait at the gate before you go out for a walk

■ **As a good safety measure,** *teach your puppy to wait on the curb before you cross the street.*

- Have him wait in a corner of the room when you carry a heavy object or hot food – things that may hurt him if they fall on him
- Have him wait at the door till you give him permission to go inside

I can't emphasize this enough: Use your puppy's training around the house. The more you use it, the better the end result.

THREE SIMPLE WAYS TO TEACH "WAIT"

Whichever way you choose to teach your puppy to wait, the two constants are: Praise him after he gets it right and correct him when he does the wrong thing, or ignores you. Never fail on these two counts.

1 Using treats

Keep some treats or a shaker. Have your puppy sit, tell him, "Dax, wait," and step away. Shake the shaker, call him to come, and back away a few steps. Praise him for coming. If he moves before you call him, tell him "Acckk!" and put him back in his original position.

2 Using a leash

Keep a treat and have your pup sitting on leash. Say "Dax, wait," and step away. Call him, use the leash to make sure he comes, and praise him when he does. Give him the treat. If he breaks the wait, say "Acckk!" Snap and release the leash. Put him back in the original position.

3 Using body language

Have your puppy sit, tell him, "Dax, wait," and step away from him. Wait a few seconds, then tell him, "Dax, OK, you can move!" and encourage him to get up with your body language (bounce up and lift your hands high). Praise him when he moves.

Teaching your puppy to respect boundaries

WITH BOUNDARY TRAINING you can teach your puppy to remain in the front yard with you (always with you, never alone) and to remain within the boundaries of the yard. You can teach him to respect the gate, the garage door, and outside doors. By teaching him to understand these boundaries, there is less chance of him dashing out through the gate or running away.

It's not easy

Boundary training is very difficult for puppies. If a cat is grooming itself just beyond the boundary of your yard, your puppy is not going to be able to resist making a dash for the cat. So why are we even trying to teach it? Because if you start teaching boundary training now, when your puppy is grown up the training will work. You just have to keep teaching, enforce the boundaries, and be patient as he grows up.

■ **Boundary training** *means teaching your puppy to respect physical boundaries such as fences, gates, or doors.*

Never rely totally on boundary training to restrain or protect your puppy until he is grown up, mentally mature, and has had constant training.

A simple way to teach boundary training

Start in a spot where the boundary is very obvious, such as a gate.

1. Put your puppy on a leash and have him sit in front of the closed gate, inside the yard. Tell him, "Dax, wait," and step up to the gate. If he moves, correct him, "Acckk!" and put him back in position

2. Open the gate. If he moves, correct him again and put him back in the position from which he started

3 If he waits, go back to him and praise him. Repeat the exercise a few times, closing the gate each time before you start again

4 When he will hold the "wait" command while you open the gate, step through the gate. If he moves, correct him and put him back

5 Continue this way, opening and closing the gate, walking through and walking back, over several days and training sessions. When your puppy is doing well and is not making any mistakes (still on leash, of course), start the exercise all over at another location – such as the garage door

Another way to teach boundary training

Sit your puppy at the gate, inside the yard.

1 Fasten a *long line* to your puppy's collar. Tie the other end to something secure in the yard, such as a tree. Have a little bit of slack in the line, but not too much

2 Tell your puppy, "Dax, wait," and open the gate. If he dashes through, let him go and hit the end of the line

3 When he does, go to him and tell him, "Well, that was dumb!" in a matter-of-fact voice

4 Walk him back to where he started, close the gate, and repeat the whole exercise

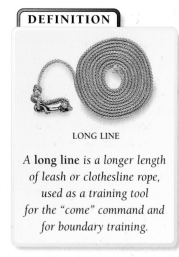

DEFINITION

LONG LINE

A **long line** *is a longer length of leash or clothesline rope, used as a training tool for the "come" command and for boundary training.*

After he's figured out that dashing won't work when you open the gate, leave him, open the gate, and walk through. When he's reliable there, move to another boundary and repeat the entire exercise.

■ **A 20-foot length** *of nylon clothesline rope fastened to your puppy's collar functions well as a long line.*

There's more you can do with "come"

"COME" IS SUCH AN IMPORTANT command, *that I like to teach it in many ways. In Chapter 16, I explained how to train your puppy to "come" to you with a shaker full of treats – emphasizing the sound and treats – and how to "come" to you on a leash, which gave the puppy no chance to ignore you. But there is more you can do with the "come" command.*

Coming from a distance

You can use "come" with the shaker to teach the puppy to come to you from a distance. This is best taught with two people in a large fenced area.

Don't have a yard? Sometimes fenced schoolyards or ballfields are available after hours, and can make good places to practice.

Have the shaker with you and some special treats that he really likes. Have one person hold the puppy as you let him sniff the treat. Walk away from him (don't say "wait" or "stay") and hold out the treat so he can see you still have it. When you're 20 or 30 yards away, bend down, open your arms, shake the shaker, and call your puppy. He should be running to you as fast as his legs can carry him. Praise him and hug him a great deal. Repeat the exercise with you holding the puppy while the other person walks away. Have him go back and forth like this two or three times.

Always quit before he's tired and before he loses interest. As he gets bigger and stronger, with more stamina, go farther away. But again, always stop while the game is still fun.

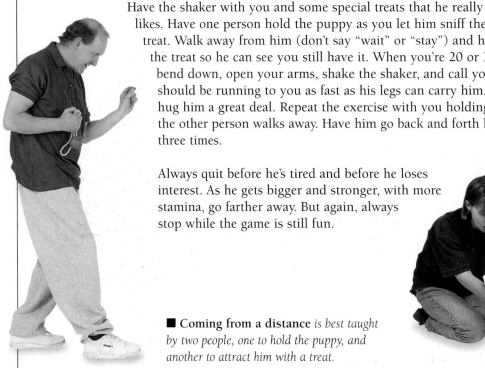

■ **Coming from a distance** *is best taught by two people, one to hold the puppy, and another to attract him with a treat.*

Practicing with distractions

When the puppy is going really well and is coming to you with no hesitation, start adding distractions.

(a) Call him when there are some kids playing on the other side of the yard, or when some kids are in-line skating outside the yard

(b) Have a family member lie on the ground (presenting an interesting distraction) while you call the puppy

(c) Have some of the puppy's toys in the grass nearby when you call him

INTERNET

www. workingdogweb.com

This is a list of links with a lot of information on testing, training, and getting started in many canine activities.

Distractions are a part of life, and your puppy must learn to ignore them. However, remember you need to set your puppy up for success. Make sure he can do what you're asking him to do.

You know your puppy better than anyone else. What distracts him? Practice with those distractions, but as you do, make sure you are also setting him up to succeed.

■ **If your puppy has trouble** *ignoring certain distractions, such as a trashcan, have him come to you on the leash for a while instead of calling him across the yard without the leash.*

Teaching "stand"

"STAND" IS NOT A DIFFICULT command to teach, but it is *very hard for puppies to do, because it requires them to stand still. The still part is hard!*

Stand-stay is hard for puppies. Do not ask him to stand for very long. Start with a few seconds, working up to maybe a minute over several weeks of training.

A SIMPLE WAY TO TEACH "STAND"

This method teaches your puppy to stand using a combination of treats and leash.

1 **Show treat**

Have your puppy on a leash. Hold it in one hand while you have a treat in the other. Ask your puppy to sit and praise him. Hold the treat in front of his nose.

2 **Lure with treat**

Tell him, "Dax, stand," and slowly pull the treat away from him so that he follows it. When he gets up onto all four paws, praise him and give him the treat. Pat his shoulder to release him.

Another way to teach "stand"

You can also help your puppy to stand without the help of treats, by using your hands. Remember to be gentle – he must not feel you are forcing or mishandling him.

1 With your puppy on a leash, ask him to sit and praise him when he does

2 Using your right hand, take hold of his collar under the neck in front of the chest. Tell him, "Dax, stand," and gently pull him forward so that he steps forward

3 As he steps forward, use your left hand under his tummy to keep him from sitting again. Praise him for standing

Once the puppy is standing easily (using either method), you can add the "stay" to it. It is then, "Dax, stand. Good to stand. Stay." When you're ready, you can go back to him, praise him and release him.

Using "stand" in real life

Once your puppy knows how to stand on command, you'll find many practical applications for "stand " in day-to-day life:

- Have your puppy stand if he's been out in the rain or has been playing in the lawn sprinklers. It's easier to towel him off when he's standing and, hopefully, standing still
- If your puppy is a breed that needs professional grooming, your groomer will appreciate it if you teach him to stand
- Your puppy will need to know how to stand nicely at the veterinarian's office, both on the scale to be weighed, and on the examination table
- If your puppy has a long coat or a thick one that needs regular combing or brushing, you can teach him to stand while you brush him

PUPPY TAILS – TRAINING CHALLENGES

I like to challenge my dogs to listen to my commands, to think, and to respond. I will tell them to sit, to lie down, or to stand, but I will give the commands in different orders. For example, I may say stand, sit, lie down, sit, stand. If he does it right, I praise him. If he has trouble, I help him. If he is doing very well, listening carefully and trying hard, I really praise him and give him some treats.

Teaching your pup "go to bed"

"GO TO BED" IS A COMMAND that is used only at home, but it's still useful. In Chapters 6, 7, 8, and 9 I discussed the uses for kennel crates and how to teach your puppy to use one. I mentioned teaching the puppy a command that means, "Go put yourself to bed," but during crate training you are always there to make sure the puppy goes into his crate and then you close the door behind him. It is very nice to be able to sit on the couch in the evening, tell your puppy, "Dax, go to bed" and have your puppy get into his crate on his own.

When to start?

You can start teaching this command by emphasizing the words as you put your puppy to bed at night. When you know he understands the words, say "go to bed" as you are walking toward his crate. If he dashes ahead to the crate, praise him. If he dashes to the crate and also puts himself inside, really praise him.

Now, start telling him earlier, first as you walk down the hall, then, as you are getting up from the couch. Always follow up by going to the crate and praising him. If you just send him to the crate, he'll come back to you looking for praise.

Don't overdo the "go to bed" command. If you do it too often (more than twice a day) your puppy will regress, lose interest or enjoyment in the crate, and will refuse to go to it.

Self-rewarding action

At some point you will see your puppy go to the crate on his own and lie down. When he's doing this the crate itself will begin to be a reward for going inside. At this point, you can start sending your puppy there without following him. However, you should still praise him.

■ **Your puppy** *will soon start to enjoy taking refuge in his crate.*

PUPPY TAILS – GOING TO BED

My dog, Kes, who at this writing is just about 2 years old, has been putting herself to bed reliably for about 16 months. When she was younger, she would go to the crate, but if I didn't close the door behind her she would come out, waiting for me to send her in again. To her it was a big game and going in and out was fun. Now she's taking her training more seriously and understands that "Go to bed" means go and stay there.

Teaching "leave it"

PUPPIES PUT EVERYTHING *in their mouths but are not very smart about it, and often it's something that could make them sick. That's why I teach the "leave it" command. I want my dogs to turn away immediately from whatever interests them when I say "Leave it!" That means if a chicken bone is on the ground, I want Kes to immediately turn away from it when she hears that command. This is hard for her, but it could save her life some day.*

A simple way to teach "leave it"

Hold your puppy's leash in one hand and some treats or a toy in the other.

1. Drop something on the ground that will get his interest and that he is normally not allowed to touch – a smelly sock, a bone, or something similar

2. Walk toward the item. When your puppy sees it and begins to move toward it, tell him, "Dax, leave it!" as you put the toy under his nose and lead him (using the toy) in the opposite direction

3. Remember to praise him and let him play with the toy

■ **Say "leave it!"** *and only then use a toy to turn your pup away from the item that attracts him, such as a bone. Otherwise he will think "leave it" is a new name for his toy.*

Bone

Toy

ANOTHER WAY TO TEACH "LEAVE IT"

Practice this training with different items so that your puppy learns that the command applies to anything you tell him to ignore.

1 Show item

Have the puppy on a leash and drop the interesting item, such as a bone, on the ground. Walk toward the item.

Bone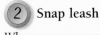

Trivia...

Most terriers are very tenacious, and once their minds are set on something, it's hard to make them stop. The "leave it" command is very important so that you can control what these dogs grab when you're out on a walk.

2 Snap leash

When your puppy sees it, tell him "leave it!" as you turn sharply away from it, snapping the leash so that he follows you.

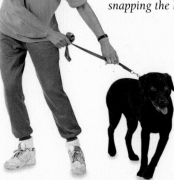

3 Give treat

As with any training, praise and treat your puppy when he has obeyed you.

What else would you like to teach?

You can teach your puppy almost anything, as long as you can communicate with him about what you want. What is important to you? What would you like him to do (or not do)? Teach him using the same techniques we've used so far.

1 Show him what to do, helping him if he needs help

2 Teach him a word (command) for it

3 Praise him when he does it right, even if you've helped him

4 Really praise him when he does it right all by himself

5 Correct him when he makes a mistake

6 After he's made a mistake, help him do it right

7 Repeat the training often

■ **Training around the house** *is very important. You'll thank yourself for it when your puppy grows into a well-behaved dog who knows his place in your daily routine.*

A simple summary

✔ The eight basic commands were just the foundation. There is a lot more you can teach your puppy.

✔ Practice the "come" command more, using new techniques. Keep it fun and exciting.

✔ Other commands can be useful around the house or out in public.

✔ Never wear out a command. Practice it enough so that your puppy understands it, but not so much that he becomes bored or frustrated.

✔ You can teach your puppy much more by using the basic training techniques you've learned so far.

Chapter 18

Using Training to Avoid Trouble

MORE DOGS ARE GIVEN UP by their owners for behavior problems than for any other reason. These problems, such as housetraining accidents, leg lifting and marking, barking, digging, or chewing are not simply bad behavior on the part of the dog. A dog's owner has a lot to do with any behaviors the dog might develop. That's why solving behavior problems requires a team approach, with both dog and owner on the team.

In this chapter...

✓ Why does my puppy do that?

✓ Common puppy problems and solutions

✓ Too much barking

✓ Mouthing and biting

✓ Let's retrace those steps

AVOID PROBLEM BEHAVIOR WITH PRECAUTIONS AND TRAINING

Why does my puppy do that?

MOST BEHAVIORS THAT ARE PROBLEMS *for us are not problems to a dog. Dogs bark because they have something to say; dig because the ground smells good or because you have gophers; chew because it's fun or because they're teething; and raid the kitchen trash because there are wonderful tidbits in there. All of these things are natural for dogs. Other things also affect problem behavior, sometimes quite significantly. Let's take a look at some of them.*

Health problems

If your dog has been well-housetrained and suddenly begins having accidents in the house, make an appointment with your veterinarian. A urinary tract infection or some kind of stomach upset can cause housetraining accidents. If the dog is in pain, she may be distracted or even aggressive. Other health concerns can trigger problem behavior too, so a thorough exam is always a good idea.

Many behaviorists and dog trainers believe at least 20 percent of all behavior problems are related to the dog's health in some way.

When you make your appointment, make sure you tell the vet that you are working on some problem behaviors and want to pin-point or eliminate any potential health problems. Don't just leave the vet guessing as to why he's examining your dog.

Lack of leadership

As I have mentioned several times, you must be your puppy's leader. If you aren't the leader, someone else needs to be – after all, there must be a leader! If you won't do it, your puppy will, especially if she has a dominant or assertive personality.

Dogs lacking leadership can develop a host of problems. Leg lifting, marking, mounting, humping, and other unacceptable behaviors are frequently seen. Aggressive behavior toward family members is common, as is destructive behavior around the house.

■ **Aggressive guarding of food** *or toys is a common problem among dogs that lack a leader.*

Setting yourself as leader

If you are not her leader your puppy can grow up into an aggressive, difficult to handle dog. If your puppy doesn't feel you are her leader, here's how you can change her opinion:

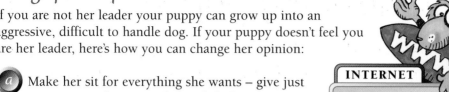

(a) Make her sit for everything she wants – give just one command to sit, and then help her do it

(b) Have her lie down and stay at your feet (with you either sitting or standing) at least twice a day

(c) Go through doorways, gates, or up and down stairs first, and make her wait for your permission

(d) Do not let her sleep in bed with you

(e) Feed her at set times, giving her food and taking it away after 15 minutes (that is, do not leave food out all the time)

(f) Do not play rough games such as tug-of-war or wrestling with her; play games such as retrieving games that make her work for you

INTERNET

www.vin.com/PetCare/
Articles/TOC/
P00075.htm

The Veterinary Information Network has a long list of questions and answers about canine behavior problems.

DEFINITION

*A **Kong** is a hard, hollow toy that looks like three rubber balls that have been squashed together. A **Buster Cube** is a plastic cube toy with an adjustable hole in one side so you can fill the cube with kibble. The dog must manipulate the cube to get the kibble out.*

KONG

Boredom

You know that saying, "Idle hands are the devil's tools." Idle paws are, too. A bored dog will get into trouble. What she does may vary – some chew, some bark, and some dig.

Increase your puppy's exercise so that she's more likely to sleep when left alone. Give her a toy before you leave: a rawhide chew, a paper bag with treats in it, a *Kong*, or a *Buster Cube*. Fill the hollow center of the Kong with peanut butter and give it to her just before you leave home. Many dogs are occupied by these toys for hours at a time. Keep your puppy's obedience skills sharp. This challenges her mind. If you are gone for long hours during the day, hire a dog walker, a neighbor, or the neighbor's teenager to come over and spend some time with your puppy.

■ **Boredom in a dog** is a manifestation of *years of natural working instincts sitting idle.*

Diet

Dog foods that are very high in protein and fat, or diets that are more than 50 percent carbohydrates, are known to cause hyperactivity in some dogs. Foods high in certain sugars and starches also cause behavior problems in some dogs. Many dogs are also very sensitive to some food coloring, preservatives, or other additives. If you suspect a food-related problem, read the label of the food you are giving your puppy.
Feed your puppy a food that does not contain a lot of sugar and artificial preservatives, colorings, and additives.

Most puppies do very well on a dry food that is about 28 percent protein and 8 to 10 percent fat. Make sure most of the protein is from meat and not from grains and cereals.

Lack of exercise

Lack of exercise causes many problems. A dog that hasn't had enough exercise may, literally, bounce off the walls. She's likely to burn up all that energy doing things you'd rather she didn't. These may include running around the house, pacing, digging, barking, and other destructive behavior.

Regular aerobic exercise can help use your puppy's excess energy and keep her weight at a healthy level. The amount of exercise needed varies: A 1-mile walk would be enough for a Miniature Dachshund, but a 5-mile jog would be better for a young Labrador Retriever.

A dog that doesn't get enough exercise has other problems, too, including health problems. Just as we are getting more sedentary, so are our dogs. Experts say that more people are overweight today than at any time in recorded history, and veterinarians say the same thing about our dogs. An overweight dog is not happy, nor is she healthy.

■ **Exercise is important** *for you as well as your puppy. In fact, exercising, training, and playing with your puppy will do your health a world of good!*

What we do to our dogs

Unfortunately, behavior problems in dogs can also arise due to their owners. Such behavior problems are often the hardest to solve, because it is very difficult for us to recognize what we are doing wrong.

Canine bad behaviour can be caused by us, our personality, and how that personality affects the relationship we have with our dogs.

Our behavior can affect our dogs in many ways:

a **Overprotective owners** take away the dog's ability to cope with the world around her. By being "protected" from everything, the dog often becomes fearful – sometimes aggressively fearful

b **Overemotional owners** who are quick to get excited or quick to react often end up with dogs just like them. Unfortunately, during episodes of excitement these dogs can get out of hand

c **Demanding owners** would prefer the dog be a furry robot that follows each and every order exactly as given. Dogs belonging to such owners never measure up

d **Overpermissive owners** don't set enough rules, and when they do set rules, they do not enforce them. These owners are not the dog's leader, and many problem behaviors can develop as a result

e **Mean owners** overpower their dogs, or make their dogs fearful or fearful-aggressive. Because aggression begets aggression in certain dogs, these owners often wind up with a dog as mean as they are

■ **A dog that cowers** *on seeing you is not expressing guilt. Either she has got used to getting a scolding from you or she's more scared of you than is good for your relationship.*

f **Shy and timid owners** tend to have dogs with one of two personality types. Many timid people get a large, extroverted dog who can project their bolder self. This dog may become over-protective of her owner, sometimes dangerously so. Alternatively, the shy owner may get a dog just like himself, and the two will go through life very quietly and fearfully

We contribute to our dog's problem behavior by training her inconsistently or incorrectly. Our dogs want to be good, and if we clearly show them what we want, they will comply.

Common puppy problems and some solutions

EVERY PUPPY *is a unique individual, just as you are. Therefore, there are no solutions that work for every person, every daily routine, and every puppy. However, over the years I have found a few solutions that do work for a great number of puppies.*

Jumping on people

One of the most common methods of correcting jumping is to knee the puppy in the chest, but I don't agree with this. It may teach the puppy to jump on her owner's back instead of in front of him, but it doesn't teach her what to do to get attention from her owner – which is why she's jumping in the first place.

Instead, teach the puppy to sit. When the puppy learns to sit for attention, quivering in anticipation of petting, she will have no need to jump on you. If you consistently reward her for sitting, the jumping will disappear.

You will also have to teach her to sit for other people and not jump on them. When she tries to jump, use a snap and release correction, and say "Acckk! No jump!" Then make her sit. Don't allow other people to pet her until she's sitting.

■ **Puppies look upon children** *as their playmates but a growing puppy can be very heavy. If she jumps on children she may do them harm.*

Dashing through doors and gates

This problem is easily solved by using the boundary training I explained in Chapter 17. Begin training your pup to wait when you open a door or gate. You can use either method, but if she tries to dash through the doors a lot, try using both methods.

Make sure everyone in the house is aware that the puppy likes to dash out, watches her and keeps her away from open doors. It is as important to teach her as to not give her opportunities to dash out while you are teaching her.

Digging

Puppies dig for a number of reasons, all of which could leave your backyard or garden looking like a war zone. To stop the digging, you need to prevent it from happening. When you're not home, don't let the puppy have free access to the lawn. Build her a dog run where she can do anything she wants! Make it big enough so she can play, make sure it's covered, and that there is water in an unspillable dish. This can be her place when you're gone. She'll be safe there and can play without getting into trouble. Then, when you're back at home, you can let her run around the backyard and when you see her start to dig (or even sniff the gopher holes), you can interrupt and teach her, "Acckk! No dig!"

■ **To correct your puppy's digging habit,** *you have to catch her in the act. Correcting her later, say, after you return home and discover her handiwork, is ineffective. It is also cruel, since she has no idea why she's being scolded.*

Controlled digging

You can control your puppy's digging by giving her a place of her own to dig, such as a spot in the yard, behind the garage, or in an out-of-the way corner. Here's how:

1. Using a shovel, loosen the dirt really well

2. Stick half a dozen dog biscuits in the dirt so they are only partially covered

3. Invite your dog to find the biscuits and to dig there

4. As she finds the biscuits, completely bury a few so that she has to dig for them, and in the beginning, help her do so

5. When she digs elsewhere, correct her and take her back to her spot

Destructive chewing

This isn't a difficult problem to solve. First, consistently correct the puppy each time she puts her mouth on something she shouldn't. Follow up each correction by handing her one of her toys. So, you show her what's wrong – "Acckk! No!" and take the wrong item away as you tell her, "Here, this is your toy. Good girl!" and hand her the toy. As a pup, she'll chew on anything so for her safety don't let her have unsupervised run of the house. Section off the garage, put away the kids' toys, the garden tools, and the pool supplies.

SIMPLE SOLUTIONS TO BAD BEHAVIOR

Changing your puppy's problem behavior requires a commitment from you. You may have to make some physical changes around the house or yard, or you may have to make some changes in your daily schedule. If you make the effort, your chances of success are greatly increased. Most canine behavior problems can be controlled if not cured. Here's how to start addressing your puppy's problem behaviors:

1. A lot of problem behavior is rooted in ill health. Make sure your puppy is healthy. Get her checked by your vet

2. Make the time to play and have fun with your dog. The time spent with you is important, and so is your laughter

3. Make sure your puppy gets enough appropriate exercise

4. Purposely arrange things so she makes a mistake when you're there to teach her

5. If your puppy is getting into a lot of trouble in the yard, build her a dog run

6. Prevent problems from occurring when you can. Put away the trash cans, pick up the children's toys, and put away the cushions for the lawn furniture

7. Teach your puppy an alternative behavior. She can't jump on you if she learns to sit for petting. She can't dash out the front door if she has been taught to sit and wait at the door

■ **If you are particular** *about your furniture, teach your pup to respect it from an early age. That's one less problem behavior for you to worry about.*

Too much barking

DOGS BARK FOR A NUMBER OF REASONS. *Protective dogs bark to warn you of trespassers – real or imagined. Social dogs bark to communicate with you and the world around them. Dogs bark at the children playing outside, the birds flying overhead, and the neighborhood dog barking down the block. Unfortunately, a barking dog is also a nuisance – sometimes a major nuisance.*

Use a squirt bottle

Start correcting barking in the house when you are close by. Make up a squirt bottle filled about an eighth of the way with white vinegar and the rest with water. Make sure the solution is primarily water with just enough vinegar so you can smell it. Any more vinegar could sting her eyes.

■ **A water pistol** *can substitute for a squirt bottle as long as the jet is not strong enough to hurt your puppy.*

If you use a squirt bottle, remember to use it on the "mist" setting, not on the "stream" setting. A hard stream could hurt your puppy if you hit her in the face or eyes.

Don't yell

When someone comes to the door and your dog barks, walk quietly to the dog and tell her "Quiet!" firmly but without yelling. Squirt the vinegar water toward her. She will smell the vinegar, stop barking, back off, and may even sneeze. Dogs have a very keen sense of smell, and very few of them enjoy the smell of vinegar. When she stops barking, tell her, "Good girl to be quiet!"

If you yell at your dog to stop barking, you're making lots of noise at the front door, which is the same thing she's doing. To your dog, you're barking too! She isn't going to stop, since she thinks you're joining in.

Barking when you are not at home

If your puppy barks when you're not home, you may have to set up a situation so you can catch her in the act. Go through all the motions of leaving: get dressed, pick up your purse, wallet or briefcase, get in the car and drive down the block. Park the car down the block and walk back with the squirt bottle in hand. When your puppy starts to bark, surprise her with "Acckk! Quiet!" and a squirt! If you set her up a few times, she will quickly learn that you have much more control than she thought.

Distractions

For a home-alone barker, take a small brown paper lunch bag and put a variety of small treats in it. You can use a slice of apple, a dog biscuit, a carrot, or a cracker with peanut butter on it. Just before you leave the house, give this to your dog. You'll have to clean up the paper bag when you get home, but your dog will be so interested in the treats, she won't even know you've left.

Special collars

A new, relatively humane anti-barking collar works with a vibration sensor. When your dog barks, it squirts a small stream of citronella in the direction of her nose. Citronella is safe, but its smell is as unpleasant to dogs as vinegar.

Don't use any of the electronic anti-bark collars for puppies, even if you feel you have a serious barking problem and would like to try one of these collars. Call a trainer or behaviorist for help instead. You never have to hurt your dog to train her.

PUPPY TAILS — BARKING UP THE RIGHT TREE

I want my dogs to warn me when people come up to the house, but I don't want problem barkers. That's why I have a 3-Bark Rule. When someone comes to the gate or door, the dogs can each respond with 3 barks. After that, I have trained them to stop. However, if there is a genuine emergency, such as the time someone tried to steal our car, they can bark as much as they like.

■ **Your puppy** *can be trained to understand that barking is desirable in some circumstances and not allowed in others.*

Mouthing and biting

WHEN YOUR PUPPY WAS with her *mother and littermates, she learned to play by wrestling. Since she doesn't have any hands, she would bite and grab her brothers and sisters. If she bit too hard, a sibling would yelp or cry and she'd back off. Using her mouth to grab something is very natural to her.*

■ **Your puppy will grow up** *to be a powerful dog with sharp teeth. A playful nip from her could turn into a serious bite.*

The most important lesson

Your puppy's teeth can easily cause you or your children harm, even though she does not mean any.

Every puppy must learn that touching teeth to skin or clothing is absolutely forbidden.

Teach this lesson right away, starting the day you bring your pup home.

1. Be consistent: Don't allow the puppy to bite you during play and then correct her for nipping in other situations

2. Don't play games that teach her to use her strength against you – no tug-of-war and no wrestling

3. Teach the children to play quietly with the puppy without running or screaming

4. Don't allow your puppy to chase the children or to "herd" them, nipping at their heels or clothing

5. Like a child, a puppy can have temper tantrums. She might throw herself around, crying, growling, or screaming, and may try to bite you. A temper tantrum is bad behavior. Do not give in. If she wants you to stop brushing her, for example, when the tantrum is over continue brushing her

Correcting the problem

There are several ways to correct mouthing and biting.

a Have the squirt bottle($\frac{1}{8}$ vinegar to $\frac{7}{8}$ water) ready in situations when you know she is apt to nip at your legs, heels, or clothes. When she does, spray her as you tell her "Acckk! No bite!" When she backs off, praise her quietly

b If she tries to mouth or bite you when you are hooking up her leash or petting her, correct her right away. With one hand, grab her buckle collar or the scruff of her neck and with the other hand simply close her mouth. Tell her firmly, "Acckk! No bite!" and do not let go of her muzzle until she take a deep sigh and relaxes. If she resists, correct her again and wait her out

Keep your cool

When you're teaching your puppy, don't lose your temper or she may try to fight you even more. When your puppy tries to mouth or bite you, keep in mind that she has to learn that it isn't acceptable to bite people. You have to teach her, and you have to be consistent with your teaching.

If you lose your temper often, your puppy's behavior may mirror your own, becoming more aggressive in response to you.

WHEN YOU NEED A TRAINER'S HELP

Don't be embarrassed to ask a trainer for help. A trainer may be able to answer your questions on the telephone, but if he says he needs to meet with you, do it. He'll charge you for the private training, of course, but if you have a problem the money will be well spent. (For references of professional trainers' organizations, see More Resources at the back of the book.) Call a trainer when:

a Your puppy bites you or any other person

b Your puppy growls at you

c Your puppy guards her food aggressively

d Your puppy regresses from previously good behavior

e Your puppy throws a temper tantrum – screaming, biting, throwing herself around – when you try to get her to do something

f You are feeling overwhelmed

g You feel as if your puppy is smarter than you

Let's go over those steps again

MORE DOGS ARE GIVEN UP by their owners for problem behavior than for any other reason. This is tragic, when so many problems can be stopped or controlled simply through training.

Questions to ask yourself

When your dog has a behavior you consider a problem, ask yourself these questions:

■ **A professional trainer** will train your puppy privately, adapting the training to your puppy's specific needs and behavior problems.

1 **Why is your dog doing this?** Try to look at it from her point of view! Is she getting enough exercise? Are you spending enough time with her? Does she have a health problem that may be causing it? Are neighborhood kids teasing her?

2 **Can you prevent the problem?** Will having a dog run help? How about a crate? Do you need to supervise her more closely?

3 **How can you teach her?** Set her up so that you can catch her in the act and correct her. Make sure you praise her if she decides to do the right thing!

4 **Does she feel leaderless?** Make sure you are your puppy's leader

5 **Is she getting enough obedience training?** Practice her obedience commands regularly and use them around the house and in your daily routine

A simple summary

✔ Problem behaviors are not a problem to the dog; to her, they are very natural behaviors.

✔ Problem behaviors happen for a reason. Try to find out why your dog is doing what she's doing.

✔ Prevent problems from happening if you can, especially when you aren't there to teach your puppy.

✔ When you are at home, teach her what is wrong and, most important, teach her what's right!

PART FIVE

DOGS LEAP AT THE CHANCE TO PLAY

Chapter 19

The Best Games and Toys

THE DIFFERENCE BETWEEN good and not so good games for your puppy lies in what they teach him. A good game teaches him lessons you want him to learn (that you are in charge, and that you are kind, fair, and caring). Bad games teach him what you'd rather not have him learn (that you are slower than him, and not as strong). Always play the good games that make your pup work for you, to do things for you that can still be fun.

In this chapter...

✔ Retrieving games

✔ Hide-and-seek games

✔ The name game

✔ What games are not good to play?

✔ What toys are good for your puppy?

Retrieving games

RETRIEVING GAMES ARE GREAT FUN, *once your puppy has learned how to retrieve. Some dogs are natural retrievers and will charge after, grab, and bring back anything that is thrown. However, some dogs need to be taught how to retrieve. Luckily, that isn't hard to do.*

Learning to retrieve

I like to use a lot of praise while teaching the retrieve, because I want the puppy to consider this fun. We are going to approach the training using very small baby steps, so that your puppy gets a lot of positive reinforcement. Use your "ice cream!" tone of voice for this activity.

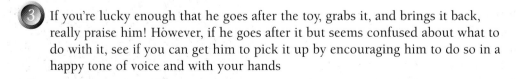

■ **Puppies invite play** *by bowing, nudging, pawing, and bringing you toys. Once your pup learns retrieving games, he'll invite you to play!*

1 Sit on the floor with your puppy. Bounce a toy around a little, so you make the puppy look at it. When he looks at it, tell him "Good!"

2 Roll the toy a few feet away. Encourage the puppy to chase after it and praise him when he does. When he goes after it, tell him "Dax, take it!"

When you start to teach your pup to retrieve, roll the toy rather than throwing it, because he can visually track a rolled toy much more easily. Watching a thrown toy is difficult for a young pup.

3 If you're lucky enough that he goes after the toy, grabs it, and brings it back, really praise him! However, if he goes after it but seems confused about what to do with it, see if you can get him to pick it up by encouraging him to do so in a happy tone of voice and with your hands

4 If he picks it up, back up a little and tell him "Bring it here!" If he does, praise him

5 Increase the distance you roll the toy very gradually. If your puppy hesitates or stops going after it, go with him to encourage him, and next time don't roll it so far

Play with the toy a little yourself to get your puppy interested in retrieving games. Right now he has no idea why you're playing the game or why you're interested in this toy.

When your puppy is going after the toy enthusiastically, start throwing it – again just short distances – and keep it exciting. As your puppy learns this game is fun and exciting, you can start playing with different toys (make sure they are safe to throw) and very gradually increase the length of the throws.

The other part of retrieving

You may come up against two hitches in teaching your puppy to retrieve:

1 **He brings the toy back but doesn't want to give it to you:** In this case take hold of the top of his muzzle and gently press his upper lips against his upper teeth as you tell him, "Dax, give!" He will open his mouth automatically and you can take the toy and praise him for giving it to you. He'll soon learn that giving up the toy means you will throw it again, and the fun of continuing the game will become his reward

2 **He likes to play "keep-away" with the toy:** Initially, if he is getting the toy but not bringing it all the way back, then play with several toys. He will drop one to get the others, and you can then just walk around the yard, picking up and throwing the various toys

■ **Dogs love to play** *outdoor retrieving games, and breeds like Golden Retriever (shown here) or Labrador Retriever are great at retrieving from water. Once you've taught your puppy how to retrieve, you can look forward to years of healthy, outdoor activity.*

Hide-and-seek games

GAMES THAT TEACH YOUR PUPPY *to use his natural scenting abilities are good for him. All dogs have these scenting abilities, and smelling the world is probably more important than seeing it for a dog.*

Hide-and-seek games also give you a chance to teach the puppy the family members' names: Go find Dad, or Mary, or Joanne, or sister. Why is this useful? Because my dogs know our names, when my husband needs a screwdriver, I can hand one to Dax and tell him, "Take it! Go find Paul!" and he'll take the screwdriver to my husband. He gets a chance to work and be praised for it, and it saves me some effort!

TEACHING HIDE-AND-SEEK

Hide-and-seek is best played with two people and the puppy.

1 One person holds the puppy

2 You keep some treats and run away to hide. Initially the hiding place must be very close and easily accessible

3 The first person tells the puppy "Go find Mom!" and lets the puppy go

4 You call out to the puppy

5 You praise him enthusiastically and give him a treat when he finds you

6 Stop calling him when he starts using his scenting abilities to find you

■ **Puppy responds to call:** *You should quietly call the puppy to encourage him.*

■ **Puppy "seeks" on his own:** *He will have his head down and his nose to the floor, rather than an "up and listening" attitude.*

Shorter-muzzled dogs, such as Shih Tzu, Pugs, and Bulldogs, are somewhat hampered in their scenting abilities. You may just have to make the scenting-based game a little easier for them.

Make it harder

As the puppy gets better at the game, make it harder. Have the person who is hiding walk around a little first, leaving a scent trail. Or go into a different room or down the hall. The game can also move outside. Dad can hide around the corner of the garage or behind some bushes. Hold onto the puppy in the front yard and Dad can go around to the back of the house. Make it more challenging but easy enough for the puppy to succeed.

The name game

WHEN YOUR PUPPY WILL RETRIEVE *a few different toys, you can teach him the name game. Your goal is to teach him to recognize the different toys by their names. If you think this is going to be very tough for the puppy, you are in for a surprise!*

■ **Dogs love playing,** *so learning a new game will not be a chore for your puppy.*

Teaching the name game

This game requires your puppy to think a lot! Keep the game simple, use lots of praise, and train in very short increments – 2 or 3 minutes at a time. Start by putting a few toys within your reach, but out of the puppy's sight.

1. Sit on the floor with the puppy and one toy. Send him after the toy, calling it by name, "Dax, get the tennis ball!" Praise him when he goes after it and again when he brings it back. Do this two or three times

2. Put the tennis ball away and bring out another toy. Send the puppy after this, again, calling it by name, "Dax, get the chew toy!" Praise him when he goes after it and when he brings it back. Do this two or three times

3. Now put the chew toy out and, with your puppy watching, roll the tennis ball past it. Tell the puppy to go after the tennis ball. If he does, praise him. If he goes after the chew toy, don't say anything (no corrections!), just start all over again

4. When he goes after the tennis ball, reverse the game, sending him after the chew toy and not the tennis ball. Be patient the first few times

■ **Choosing among many toys** *does not confuse a puppy. If you teach him patiently, your puppy will learn that a specific sound pertains to a specific toy and he'll start choosing the one you ask for.*

Adding more toys

When the puppy has figured out how to play the game with two toys, add another toy. Teach the puppy this toy's name just as you did with the first two toys. When your puppy understands that one, add another toy. After three toys, you will find your puppy catching on very quickly.

Later, when your puppy is grown up – long past puppyhood – and is reliable around the house, teach him other words. Teach your adult dog to find your car keys, the television remote, your cellular phone, and anything else that you use (and lose!) regularly.

Don't teach your puppy to find things, like your glasses, which could injure him if he bites down on them.

■ **Teach your puppy** *to retrieve specific objects, and you could have instant mail and newspaper delivery for many years to come!*

What games are not good to play?

SOME GAMES TEACH *your puppy things it's better that he doesn't know. For example, to your puppy, the leader is the one who is the biggest, strongest, fastest, and smartest, or the one who thinks he is! If you play games that teach your puppy that you are not as strong as he is or not very fast, he could seriously start doubting your leadership abilities.*

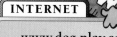

INTERNET

www.dog-play.com

You'll find descriptions of a wide variety of dog sport and games, and links to other pages with more information.

Don't teach your puppy games that teach him to use his strength against you. He could learn to physically struggle against you — a bad lesson. Your puppy might then struggle against you any time you want him to do something he doesn't want to do.

Wrestling

One game that is very popular with most puppies and almost all boys and young men is wrestling. Puppies wrestle a lot with each other in the litter. However, when growing puppies wrestle with their owners, they learn to use their strength and, often, their teeth against people. They learn to fight you, to resist you, and even to hurt you. Wrestling is never a good game to play with a puppy.

■ **Wrestling teaches** *young puppies body coordination, and develops their reflexes and strength. But that's strictly between puppies. You must not get involved in wrestling matches with your pup.*

■ **Most dogs enjoy tug-of-war** *games and the games are usually friendly – although there can be some growling as the dogs use their strength against one another.*

Tug-of-war

Dax and Kes, my two Australian Shepherds, like to play tug-of-war together and will pull each other back and forth. This is fine. They are evenly matched and are playing much more naturally than they could ever play with me. However, when a puppy plays tug-of-war with his owner, the owner usually gets tired of the game first and drops the toy, allowing the dog to get it. What did that teach the puppy? That if he fights enough and tries hard enough, he will win! Again, a bad lesson for the puppy to learn.

Think about the games you play

When you're playing with your puppy, try to think about what the game is teaching your puppy. It's hard to do, but try to think about the game from your puppy's perspective. Are you teaching him that it's permissible to fight you, use his strength against you, growl at you, or nip you? If you are allowing him to jump on the middle of your chest now when he's 10 pounds, are you still going to like it in 8 months when he's some 60 pounds of hard muscle?

Don't play any game with your puppy that encourages any aspect of behavior that you will be uncomfortable with when he is full-grown.

Trivia...

Konrad Lorenz, the Nobel Prize-winning expert on animal behavior, said that play develops a dog's mind. By stimulating the dog's mind during play, you can actually create a more intelligent dog. That's another reason to play good games with your puppy.

What toys are good for your puppy?

JUST AS THERE ARE good and bad games to play with your puppy, there are good and bad toys. Unlike games, toys by themselves don't usually give a puppy a wrong message. Instead, bad toys are usually considered bad because they're dangerous to the puppy. Balls that are small enough to be inhaled or swallowed are obviously dangerous, as are toys that come apart easily with small pieces that can be swallowed, or toys made from substances that are dangerous or poisonous.

Tennis balls

Tennis balls bounce well, are easy to throw and, most important, are soft on the teeth and big enough that they are not a choking danger for most dogs.

For smaller breeds, such as those in the Toy group, small balls that are just as soft and bouncy are manufactured for cats to play with. You'll find plenty of them at pet supply stores. Just make sure whatever ball you buy is big enough that your small dog can't swallow it.

■ **A tennis ball** *can keep a puppy occupied for hours.*

If you have a very big dog, even a tennis ball may be too small to play with. As your puppy grows up, switch to a larger ball if it seems that the dog could accidentally inhale or swallow the tennis ball.

Other retrieving toys

There are a variety of toys made for dogs to retrieve. Some, such as soft fabric flying disks, are great toys. Canvas dummies – like the ones used to train retrieving bird dogs – also make good toys. If your dog likes to retrieve, browse through the shelves at your local pet supply store and see what's available.

Kongs

Kong toys are a lot of fun for dogs, and are safe. A Kong looks like a hard rubber snowman or three balls (small, medium, and large) squashed together. Kongs come in different sizes, and there is an appropriate size for every dog.

Kongs are hollow inside, and if you fill that hollow space with peanut butter or soft cheese, you can keep a puppy occupied and out of trouble for a long time. These toys are also great for retrieving games, because they bounce every which way.

■ **Make sure** *that your puppy's kong is big enough so that he can't swallow it or choke on it.*

The Buster Cube

The Buster Cube is a big plastic cube that is about 5 inches square on each side and looks like a box. On one side of the cube there is a hole with an adjustable opening.

In a Buster Cube, you can open the hole and fill the cube with dry dog food, then adjust it to spill out a lot or just a few pieces of food each time the dog knocks the cube over.

When you first introduce the dog to the cube, you can have it wide open so the dog gets a lot of reinforcement for knocking this around. Later, when he knows that goodies come out of it, you can adjust it so fewer treats come out. This will keep dogs occupied for hours on end, especially those that are very fond of food.

Chew toys

Chew toys are very necessary for puppies, especially when they are teething. They are also needed to help teach the puppy what is right and what is wrong for him to chew on. You need to be able to take away your things and hand him something he is allowed to and wants to chew on.

Don't give your pup anything to chew on that you won't want him to be chewing on later. If you give him an old shoe to play with, he'll think chewing shoes is permissible. You don't want him to chew your new shoes, do you?

Rawhide chews

Rawhide chews are popular chew toys, both at the pet supply store and with my dogs. However, I have to be very careful with rawhides, because several of my dogs like to chew off big pieces and try to swallow those pieces whole.

RAWHIDE CHEWS

To keep your puppy safe, only allow him to chew on rawhides when you can supervise him.

OTHER EDIBLE CHEWS

Other edibles

You must use caution with other edible chews as well. The pig ears, snouts, hooves, and other edible chew treats are extremely popular, and dogs seem to gobble them up – literally! However, some of these are very brittle, especially the pig ears, and I would be concerned about those brittle pieces in a puppy's mouth, throat, and digestive tract. After giving your puppy any chew toy, examine his stools carefully for pieces of the chew toy coming through. In addition, if your puppy is passing blood or stops passing stools, get him in to the vet right away.

The key to choosing safe chew toys is to find something your puppy will chew on without detaching small pieces. Many of the hard rubber toys, such as Kongs and Nylabones, are great for this.

A simple summary

✔ There are good games that teach your puppy lessons you want him to learn, and bad games that teach him things he should not learn.

✔ Retrieving, hide-and-seek, and the name game are all good. Tug-of-war and wrestling are not good games to play.

✔ The Buster Cube, Kong toys, and retrieving toys are good, safe toys for your puppy.

✔ Give your puppy edible chew toys only when you are there to supervise him, and use them with caution or he may choke on them.

Chapter 20

Why Does My Puppy do That?

MANY DOG OWNERS ARE DISGUSTED to see their dog drink water out of the toilet bowl or eat feces from the cat's litterbox. "How can she do that?" they ask in horror! Well, dogs are not people, and their behavior can be very different from ours. Because dog owners don't know why dogs do these things, the behaviors cause misunderstanding between dog and owner. Sometimes nobody knows why dogs do what they do, but we can make educated guesses.

In this chapter...

✓ Understanding canine body language

✓ Understanding the canine physique

✓ Strange quirks of canine behavior

✓ Other confusing canine stuff

BUT WE ALL MAKE MISTAKES SOMETIMES!

Understanding your puppy's body language

DOGS DO USE THEIR VOICES to communicate, and most dog owners recognize several different types of barks and whines their dogs use in different situations. But when it comes to language, dogs use their bodies best. Your dog conveys a wealth of information with her body language, and it's a language you can definitely learn.

> **DEFINITION**
>
> **Body language** consists of positions of the body, of body parts, and facial expressions; dogs use canine body language to communicate.

WHY DOES MY DOG WAG HER TAIL?

Tail wagging is the most unique act associated with dogs. Although most people interpret a wagging tail as a sign of happy dog, a wag usually has a more subtle meaning. With most dogs, a wagging tail is a sign of strong emotion. With all strong emotions (including happiness), the tail wag is part of a complex set of physical signs that can also involve the body, ears, nose, eyes, and mouth.

a Feeling dominant

When your dog feels strong and dominant she'll lean forward, her tail held high and wagging slowly from side to side.

b Feeling happy

When your dog is happily greeting you, her tail will be lower than the hips and will be wagging wildly.

c Feeling worried

When your dog feels worried or submissive, she'll crouch with her tail between her back legs; only the tip will be wagging.

Tailless dogs often twitch their stub just as if they had a tail, or they wag their entire back end.

Why does she lower her front end when she wants to play?

When a puppy (or an adult dog) lowers her front end, including the head and shoulders, leaving her hips high, it's called a play bow. This body language is an invitation to play, and is used by dogs, wolves, coyotes, and many of the other canine species. Puppies will use the play bow when they want their littermates to play with them. They'll also use it to invite adult dogs and their human playmates, including you.

If you wish to invite your puppy to play, you can use the same body language. Lift your hands high, then bring them down in front of you, making a bowing motion.

Why does she pant when she isn't hot?

Dogs pant to lose heat. With her big, wet tongue hanging out, a dog can lose a lot of heat through evaporation. Since dogs do not sweat anywhere except on the pads of their feet, this cooling process is very important. Panting can also be a sign of stress. When she's in a situation that bothers her for any reason, your dog may begin to pant. If she anticipates something bad happening at the veterinarian's office, your dog may pant even though the air conditioning is on in the office.

Remember, too, that just because you aren't hot doesn't mean your dog isn't. Your dog may begin panting to lose heat even while you're still comfortable. Keep in mind, she's wearing a fur coat and can't sweat.

Why does she yawn when she's not tired?

Yawning when a dog is not sleepy is what is called a calming signal. If, during your training sessions for example, your puppy looks away from you and yawns, she is trying to tell you to calm down. Apparently she is feeling stress, either from herself or from you, and she's trying to relieve it.

Other calming signals that dogs give include eye blinking, sneezing, looking away, and scratching. So if your puppy begins scratching at her collar during training sessions, she is also telling you to calm down.

■ **A puppy,** *feeling the stress of weighty matters, may calm herself with a yawn.*

Understanding your puppy's physique

THE WAY DOGS BEHAVE *has a lot to do with how they are built and how they perceive the world. While we probably rely most on our sense of sight for information about the world around us, dogs depend on their senses of smell and hearing – which are much, much keener than ours. It's one reason why they sometimes seem to be reacting to nothing – it's only nothing to us. Moreover, their digestive systems often compel them to make choices that seem strange to us. And their reproductive systems exert powerful forces on their behavior.*

How well do dogs smell?

We can't even imagine how well dogs smell the world around them. For example, we think salt is odorless, but a trained scenting dog can discriminate between a bucket of plain water and one that has one teaspoon of salt dissolved in it. That is amazing! This ability is why dogs are used so frequently by law enforcement agencies to detect drugs and other illegal substances, bombs, and even animals and animal products that are being transported illegally.

A dog's nose has over 200 million scent-receiving cells and a large part of her brain is devoted to interpreting scent. A trained scenting dog's nose is more accurate than any machine yet built by humans.

■ **Smelling** *is your dog's way of gathering information about the world around her. She can smell things you will never be able to discern.*

Why does my dog roll in stinky stuff?

This is another habit that puzzles many dog owners. Why does a dog roll herself in cow manure, rotting carcasses, or other stinky stuff? Although the dogs can't tell us why, some experts say that many predators, including dogs, roll in filth to help disguise their scent. Other experts say the dog may simply like a particular scent, for whatever reason. Some dogs will roll in cat urine, some will roll on tobacco products, and others appear attracted to petroleum products. Some dogs don't roll in anything! It just seems to be a personal fragrance statement some dogs make.

■ **Dogs often cover themselves** *in foul-smelling stuff – despite their sensitive noses!*

Why does she lick her genitals?

Although licking the genitals is not all that attractive from a human perspective, it is a natural action for your puppy. Cleanliness is important to continued good health, and your puppy licks herself to keep herself clean. Occasionally in a male dog, this behavior will progress from simple cleaning to self pleasure. If this happens, you can stop the behavior with a verbal correction, especially if it occurs in public.

Why does she scoot her rear end on the ground?

This behavior is related to the anal glands. When these glands get full, they become sore and uncomfortable. A dog will sit down and drag herself using her front legs so that they are scratched on the ground. Sometimes this is enough to express or empty the glands.

If the full anal glands of a dog are not relieved, they can become infected and impacted, sometimes badly enough to require surgery. If your dog is scooting her rear on the ground, you should take her to see your veterinarian.

A dog dragging her rear on the ground could also have intestinal worms. Watch her stool for rice-like segments of tapeworms, or take a stool sample to your vet for analysis.

■ **Many dogs** *eat grass with as much enthusiasm as they eat meat or other treats.*

Why does my pup eat grass?

For many years, experts believed dogs ate grass to induce themselves to vomit, since some dogs do vomit after eating grass. However, most dogs don't seem to have any trouble vomiting, and will do so whenever something doesn't settle well in their stomach, so that explanation doesn't seem to make much sense.

When given a chance, many dogs will eagerly consume tomatoes, green beans, strawberries, apples, carrots, grapes, and many other fruits and vegetables, especially sweet ones. There's probably no hidden reason behind this behavior except sheer liking.

Although scientifically classified as carnivores, dogs behave like omnivores – animals that consume both animal and plant matter.

If my puppy's nose is not cold and wet, does it mean she is sick?

A dog's nose feels cold because of the moisture that evaporates off it. Her body temperature is actually higher than ours, so if there is no evaporation, her nose will feel warm.

Your puppy's nose should not be dry and chapped. If it is, consult your veterinarian.

Do big feet on a puppy mean she'll be very big as an adult?

It has long been said that a puppy with big feet will grow up to be a big dog. This is usually correct, but not always. In reality, big feet seem to signify that the puppy has lots of what is commonly called "bone." She may grow up to be a big dog, or she may grow up to be a medium-size dog with heavy bone, or thick legs and feet.

To tell how big your pup will grow up to be, take a look at her parents if you can. That'll give you an idea of her adult size.

Strange quirks of your puppy's behavior

ALL DOGS DO THINGS *that just don't seem to make sense – to us. However, dogs are sensible animals, and everything they do has a very good reason to them. We can try to understand things from our dogs' perspective.*

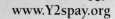

INTERNET

www.Y2spay.org

Check this site for questions on spaying or neutering. Some typical canine sexual behavior can be stopped with these.

When my husband gives me a hug and a kiss, why does my puppy try to get between us?

Ah, jealousy! Your puppy sees that someone is getting attention and affection other than her, and she just wants her share. It doesn't matter how much you give her, she'll probably still try to get in between the two of you. That's just how jealousy works. You can, however, correct the behavior. Don't let the puppy run your life, or worse yet, ruin your love life!

As your puppy becomes an adult, her jealous behavior can change into a protective one. And a dog that tries to protect you from your husband can be a real problem.

Why do dogs smell each others' rear ends?

Dogs have scent glands on either side of the anus that produce a smell that is unique to each dog. These anal glands contain a material that is expressed in small amounts each time the dog has a bowel movement. When greeting each other, dogs will take a sniff at these glands to get to know each other better. Think of this as a personal perfume!

Why does she try to smell my crotch?

Just as with another dog, it's where your calling card is for a scent-driven animal. Your puppy will have no social taboos about the crotch area – in fact, to her that will be a very natural place to sniff. For many puppies, the crotch is nose height, so it's just convenient.You can, of course, give her a correction every time she tries to sniff you or other people there. Use your voice, tell her "Acckk! No sniff!" and move her nose away. She'll soon get the idea.

Why does she eat the cat's feces?

Ah, the cat litter candy problem! Cats are true carnivores, and evolved to eat prey – the whole prey, including skin, small bones, meat, and guts. Commercial cat food includes meat but also contains grain and grain products that cats usually do not digest well. Therefore, cats are often passing through only partially digested food. Your puppy, smelling this, thinks this is a wonderful treat!

Moreover, when she helps himself and you get all excited, it becomes a really special treat for her because, after all, you are excited!

Put the litterbox someplace where the cats can get into it but the puppy can't. Or get a covered box, and make sure the puppy can't get in. Prevention is the cure here, because you aren't going to change your cats' digestive system, and the puppy is going to continue to search for kitty treats.

■ **Don't leave cat feces** *lying around where your pup might find it. If she sees it, she will eat it!*

Why does she eat her own feces?

This problem is most often seen in puppies under 6 months old. Nobody is sure why they do this, but some of the common theories are that the puppy has a vitamin or mineral deficiency, or internal parasites, or is simply bored or hungry. Here's what you can do:

a Ask your vet if he or she can give you something to feed your puppy that will make her stool distasteful to her (you already thought it was, right?)

b Increase the fiber in her diet

c Be sure to pick up after your puppy as quickly as possible after she eliminates

Eating her own feces is not a healthy habit for your puppy. It can lead to vomiting, diarrhea, and internal parasites.

Why does she bury the bone I give her?

Burying bones probably has its roots in hunting behavior. When survival depended upon what was caught during the hunt, every scrap of meat was important to a dog pack and they buried the leftovers. This hid it from other predators and preserved it for future use.

Why does she drink out of the toilet?

Your dog drinks out of the toilet to get a drink. It's that simple. The water in the toilet is sometimes colder, cleaner, and fresher than the water in her dish. She doesn't think about what happens in the toilet before she went there for some water, and she has no social taboos about it. She just wants a drink!

If you use drop-in toilet cleaners, always keep the lid down. These products are poisonous.

She has lots of toys, so why does she still chew on my stuff?

You may have given your puppy too many toys. If a puppy is surrounded by toys, she thinks everything is her's and she can play with and chew on everything. However, if you limit her toys and only give her two or three at a time, she learns that only some things are her's. Take away a few of her toys. When she touches something of yours, let her know that's wrong, "Acckk! No!" Take it away and hand her one of her toys, "This is yours!"

Keep in mind, too, that your puppy may be chewing on your stuff because it's yours and she likes your smell (which is on the stuff). With these puppies, prevention is the key. Put your stuff away and don't let your puppy have too much freedom around the house.

Why does my puppy steal the toilet paper?

Some dogs just love to grab the end of the toilet paper roll and run with it all over the house. Others love the pop of a tissue as it is pulled out of the box. This behavior is more common in females, and may be related to their instinct to build a nice, comfy nest for their own puppies.

Sometimes puppies do things just to get your attention. If you see your pup reaching for a tissue and shout and start grabbing for her, that's a really fun game for her, and you've just joined in! The best way to deal with this problem is simply to prevent it. Keep the bathroom door closed, and move the tissue box to a higher shelf. If you do catch your puppy in the act, give her a matter-of-fact correction. Say "Acckk! No!" and redirect her attention to some appropriate toy.

■ **Unspayed females** *are prone to stealing toilet paper and shredding it – are they nest building?*

Other confusing canine stuff

MYTHS ABOUND CONCERNING DOGS, *how they behave, and what's good for them. Your neighbors tell you one thing, your mother tells you another, and your friend tells you a third. Who should you listen to? Your dog's breeder, your veterinarian, and your trainer.*

Trivia...
When your dog walks in circles before lying down, she's tamping down the grass! Not really, of course, but some instinct remains of dogs' wild days on the plains. Your puppy is rearranging her bed to make sure it's comfortable, as dogs have done for thousands of years.

IS 1 DOG YEAR EQUAL TO 7 HUMAN YEARS?

A 1 year-old dog is as mature mentally, physically, and sexually as a 16-year-old human. After that, each year of a dog's life is roughly equal to about 5–7 years of a human life. Generally speaking, the smaller the dog, the longer it tends to live.

a **Toy breeds**

Toy breeds live for a long time. They may be active at 12 and not considered old until they are 14 or 15. A Pomeranian, for example, grows up to 11in (28cm) and lives for up to 15 years.

POMERANIAN

b **Medium or large breeds**

Medium and large-sized dogs may live to age 12 or 14. Beagles, 16in (41cm) at their tallest, have a life expectancy of 13 years.

BEAGLE

c **Giant breeds**

The giant breeds, such as Newfoundlands, St. Bernards, and Mastiffs, age much more quickly and are considered old by the time they reach 8. A Spanish Mastiff, which grows up to 32in (82cm) in height, lives for only 10 years.

MASTIFF

Will a choke-type training collar hurt her?

I have discussed various types of collars on pp.195–196. Basically, most puppies start training with a flat buckle collar that doesn't slip or tighten, and is right for most puppies. However, a training collar (also called a choke chain) requires some precautions but will not hurt your puppy if it is used properly.

Always take the training collar off your puppy when you're not closely supervising her. Never allow her to pull the collar tight, and don't try to hold her in place with the collar, which also pulls it tight. If she's gasping or choking, the collar is too tight and is not being used correctly.

This collar works with a snap and release correction – just enough snap to tighten on the neck, with an immediate release. The snap of the leash must be appropriate to the size and age of your puppy. It should tighten and release just enough so that your puppy looks at you in response. Most of the effect comes from the sound of the chain rubbing against the metal ring. Use the snap as you tell the dog what she did wrong. And always accompany it with a verbal correction.

■ **A choke chain,** *or training collar, will tighten around your puppy's neck if you snap the leash.*

Why does she pull on the leash even though it hurts her?

Puppies aren't people, even though we've made them part of our family, and they don't think like people. Your puppy is often so focused on going somewhere to see something that she isn't thinking about the discomfort on her neck. That's why you need to teach the puppy to walk properly, so she can go places without choking herself.

Why can't she sleep with me?

There is no reason why your puppy can't sleep in the bedroom with you, but she needs her own bed. After all, it's your house, you are taking the place of her mother, and you must be her leader as well as her friend.

Puppies sleep with their littermates, who are their equals. They do not sleep with their mother, who is their leader. Therefore, you need your bed and your puppy needs her's.

My puppy is fine at home; why do we need to take her to puppy class?

Puppy class is not just for "bad" puppies, it's for all puppies. I'm sure there is still more you can learn, even though your puppy is good, and the instructor can teach you as well as your puppy.

The socialization at puppy class is very important. Your puppy will learn to get along with lots of different dogs and people, and to feel comfortable and follow your commands in a wide variety of situations.

I'm trying to train my puppy, but she doesn't pay attention!

There are several things that could be happening:

1. First of all, does your puppy get enough exercise? If not, paying attention to you could be hard

2. Does she get enough time with you when you aren't trying to train her? Play time, time for grooming, and cuddle time are all important

3. When you are training, use some really good food treats to teach the puppy to pay attention

4. Keep the training sessions short and sweet, so you aren't asking more than she can give you

WIGGLE WORMS!

Most puppies, like most small children, have short attention spans, but Labrador Retriever puppies are absolute wiggle worms! Keep training sessions short, use food treats and lots of praise, and make sure these guys get enough exercise.

About 5 minutes of training at a time is enough for most young pups.

LABRADOR RETRIEVER PUPPY

I want to chain her in the backyard, but my neighbor says that's cruel. Why?

If you need to restrict or contain your puppy, build a dog run – an enclosed, fenced area – for your puppy rather than chaining her. A chained dog is restricted yet vulnerable. She can't get away should a stray dog decide to torment or tease her. Even in a small dog run, she is protected by the fence.

A chained dog also gets very frustrated at her limited movement, and this can cause aggression or other problem behaviors. If a small child walks within her reach, the child could bear the brunt of her frustration, getting seriously hurt or even killed.

■ **No dog can live happily** *out in the yard all day. A dog is a pack animal, and needs to be with her pack – that's you. Without you, your puppy will become lonely, bored, frustrated, and depressed.*

A simple summary

✔ Puppies do things for a reason. We may not understand the reason, but they do.

✔ Dogs aren't people, and their body language, instincts, and behavior are different.

✔ A dog's senses and physical make-up greatly affect how she perceives the world.

✔ It's important to know as much about our dogs, their behaviors, and needs, as we can, so that we can make both our lives and theirs more enjoyable.

✔ If any of the canine behaviors escalate into aggression against a person or against any other dog, it's time to call in a professional trainer.

More Canine Resources

All-breed organisations

American Kennel Club
5580 Centerview Dr.
Raleigh
NC 27606
(919) 233-9767
www.akc.org

Canadian Kennel Club
89 Skyway Ave
Suite 100
Etobicoke
ON M9W 6R4
(416) 675-5511
www.ckc.ca

United Kennel Club
100E Kilgore Rd.
Kalamazoo,
MI 49001
(616) 343-9020
www.uckdogs.com

Health-related groups

National Animal Poison Control
Center (US only)
24-hour hotline:
(888) 426-4435

Canine Eye Registration
Foundation
South Campus Courts
Bldg. C
Purdue University
West Lafayette
IN 47907
(317) 494-8179
www.vet.purdue.edu/
~yshen/cerf.html

Humane Society of
Canada
347 Bay Street
Suite 806
Toronto
ON M5H 2R7
1-800-641-5436
www.humanesociety.com

Orthopedic Foundation
for Animals
2300 Nifong Blvd.
Columbia
MO 65201
(573) 442-0418
www.offa.org

PennHip/International Canine
Genetics
271 Great Valley Pkwy.
Malvern
PA 19355
(800) 248-8099
www.vet.upenn.edu/
pennhip/

Training-related groups

Association of Pet Dog Trainers
PO Box 385
Davis
CA 95617
(800) PET-DOGS
www.apdt.com

Canadian Association of Professional Pet Dog Trainers
PO Box 59011
Whitby
ON L1N 3V9
1-877-SIT-STAY
(Canada only)
www.cappdt.ca

National Association of Dog Obedience Instructors
729 Grapevine Highway
Suite 369
Hurst
TX 76054
www.nadoi.org

A few good books and magazines

The Consumer's Guide to Dog Food
Liz Palika
Howell Book House

The Dog Owner's Home Veterinary Handbook, 3rd Edition
James Giffin, MD and Liisa Carlson, DVM
Howell Book House

Mother Knows Best: The Natural Way to Train Your Dog
Carol Lea Benjamin
Howell Book House

Natural Dog Care
Bruce Fogle, DVM
Dorling Kindersley Publishing Inc.

The New Encyclopedia of the Dog
Bruce Fogle, DVM
Dorling Kindersley Publishing Inc.

Dog & Kennel
7-L Dundas Circle
Greensboro
NC 27407
(336) 292-4047
www.dogandkennel.com

Dog Fancy
PO Box 6500
Mission Viejo
CA 92690
(714) 855-8822
www.animalnetwork.com/dogs/

Dog World
PO Box 6500
Chicago
IL 60680
(312) 609-4340
www.dogworldmag.com

AKC Gazette
American Kennel Club
260 Madison Avenue
New York
NY 10016
(212) 696-8314

Dogs in Canada
Canadian Kennel Club
89 Skyway Avenue
Suite 200
Etobicoke
ON M9W 6R4
(416) 798-9778
www.dogsincanada.com

Dogs in Cyberspace

THERE'S A LOT of information available on the Internet for dog owners. Typing "dogs" into a search engine will lead to thousands and thousands of entries. However, if you type in specific terms, such as breed, or "dog training, competition" or "dog training, pets," you'll get more specific items of interest. A word of warning, however. Do not accept everything that is written on the Internet as expert opinion. Anyone can write their opinion on a web page or a bulletin board, and they are not always right. And pages sponsored by companies that sell dog supplies obviously have business to do. Consider the source, take everything with a grain of salt and don't hesitate to ask more questions.

acmepet.petsmart.com/canine/genetic/article/primer.html

Try this site for a good overview of canine genetics. AcmePet also has many other articles about canine health and behavior.

www.akc.org

The American Kennel Club offers a breeder referral service. The site also has a wide variety of information about purebred dogs, including national breed clubs, rescue coordinators and rules for AKC-sanctioned dog sports.

www.altvetmed.com

This is the main page for links to alternative veterinary associations.

www.animalcare.ca

The official site of the veterinary profession in Canada offers a lot of information about dog care, including vaccinations, disease, behavior, and nutrition.

www.apdt.com

This is the home page of the Association of Pet Dog Trainers. You can find a trainer in your area, or find out which books or videos their trainers recommend.

www.arba.org

The home page of the American Rare Breed Association.

www.avma.org

The American Veterinary Medical Association site offers information for veterinarians and general pet care articles.

www.avma.org/netvet.default.htm

NetVet and the Electronic Zoo provide veterinary medical and animal-related online resources.

www.canidae.com

The makers of Canidae foods list the ingredients that are in their foods, and other interesting information.

www.canismajor.com/dog/guide

The Dog Owner's Guide has a wide variety of articles about puppies and dogs and links to even more.

www.cappdt.ca

This is the website for the Canadian Association of Professional Pet Dog Trainers. You can find dog training articles, links, and information about the organization membership.

www.celebritydogs.com

Think your dog has what it takes to be a star? Check out this web site for budding canine actors. It includes training tips.

www.cvma-acmv.org

The Canadian Veterinary Medical Association is a great site for vets and offers general tips about pet care.

www.cyberpet.com/cyberdog/articles/

For tips on pet-proofing your home, especially during the holidays, check out the articles on Cyberpet.

www.dmoz.org/Recreation/Pets/Dogs/Origins/

Try this site for a really interesting collection of articles about the history and evolution of dogs.

www.doctordog.com/dogbook/dogch01.html

Doctor Dog's Emergency Section offers illustrated advice on what to do in a variety of emergencies, from burns to electrocution to shock.

www.doghause.com

A fun site that has dog cartoons, quotes, stories, and more.

www.doginfomat.com/pmdd.htm#top

For a long list of links to everything you ever wanted to know about dogs in law enforcement and the military, visit this site.

www.dog-play.com

You'll find descriptions of a wide variety of dog sport and games, and links to other pages with more information.

www.dogs.about.com

This huge site is full of information about everything canine, and includes many links to other web sites.

www.doglogic.com/vaccinemain.htm

This page, written by Jean Dodds, DVM, looks at some of the controversies surrounding the traditional annual vaccination schedule.

www.fci.be/english/

The home page of the FCI, the largest international purebred dog association. If you're up to it, you can also view this page in French, German, or Spanish.

www.friskies.com

The makers of Alpo and Mighty Dog foods list the ingredients that are in their foods, and other interesting information.

www.healthypet.com

This site, maintained by the American Animal Hospital Association, includes pet care tips and an extensive library.

www.hillspet.com

The makers of Science Diet foods list the ingredients that are in their foods, and other important information.

www.hsus.org/programs/government/state_leg_up.html

The Humane Society of the United States keeps a database of all pending federal and state legislation pertaining to animals. You may or may not agree with their position, but this web site will keep you up to date either way.

www.iamsco.com

The makers of Iams and Eukanuba foods list the ingredients that are in their foods, and other information that may be of interest.

www.legacy-by-mail.com

For clickers, whistles, and training treats, as well as collars, leashes, training books, videos, and tips from top trainer Terry Ryan, check out Legacy's on-line catalog.

www.nadoi.org

This is the home page of the The National Association of Dog Obedience Instructors. They can help you find a trainer in your area.

www.napcc.aspca.org

This is the site of the US National Animal Poison Control Center. It includes advice on how to avoid poisoning, and what to do if your pet is poisoned. There is also a 24-hour hotline service: (888) 426-4435.

www.nashelter.org/crate.html

There's information in this site on crate training your dog.

www.naturesrecipe.heinzpetproducts.com

The makers of Nature's Recipe foods list the ingredients that are in their foods, and other interesting information.

www.nutroproducts.com

The makers of Nutro foods list the ingredients in their foods.

www.offa.org

The Orthopedic Foundation for Animals (OFA) maintains a registry of dogs that have been X-rayed for hip and elbow dysplasia. Breeders can then research the lists and eliminate from their breeding plan any dog that has or has produced dogs with unsound elbows and/or hips.

www.pedigree.com

The makers of Pedigree foods list the ingredients that are in their foods, and other food-related information.

www.petfinder.org

Pet Finder lists pets by type and characteristics, and by location. You can search for the perfect pet for you, or browse the pets available for adoption at a local shelter.

www.1888pets911.org

Pets 911 has information on pets that are available for adoption in your area. Just type in your zip code and they'll find you a shelter puppy.

www.pogopet.com

The Pogopet site has a variety of health-related features, including Ask the Vet and Symptom Centers that help explain why your pet may not be feeling well. There are also sections on legal issues, pet etiquette and trivia. Pogopet information can be customized for your particular pets.

www.purina.com

The makers of Purina foods list the ingredients that are in their foods.

www.takeyourpet.com

This site lists thousands of pet-friendly lodgings and local resources for pets in many cities.

www.tamebeast.com/index.html

The Tame Beast is a huge clearing house for links to other companion animal sites You'll find your way to everything doggie here.

www.ukcdogs.com

The United Kennel Club recognizes even more breeds than the AKC!

www.vet.purdue.edu/~yshen/cerf.html

The Canine Eye Registration Foundation (CERF) maintains a directory of dogs whose eyes have been examined by a licensed veterinary ophthalmologist. Thus, breeders can eliminate from their breeding program dogs with eye defects such as progressive retinal atrophy or dogs that have produced puppies that later developed eye defects.

www.vet.upenn.edu/pennhip/

PennHip, a private organization affiliated with the University of Pennsylvania Veterinary School, also maintains a registry of dogs that have been X-rayed for hip and elbow dysplasia. PennHip's registry is not as extensive as OFA's because it is newer, but some veterinarians believe the PennHip system is more acurate.

www.vin.com/PetCare/Articles/TOC/P00075.htm

The Veterinary Information Network has a long list of questions and answers about canine behavior problems.

www.wolfpark.org

To learn more about wolves, visit Wolf Park. This wildlife education and research facility studies wolf behavior.

www.wonderpuppy.net/canwehelp/index.htm

This site, called Can We Help You Keep Your Pet?, offers links to a wide variety of pages that deal with common canine (and feline) problems, such as aggression, housetraining, barking, and destructiveness.

www.workingdogweb.com

This is a list of links with a lot of information on testing, training, and getting started in many canine activities.

www.wysong.net

The makers of Wysong foods list the ingredients that are in their foods, and other interesting information.

www.Y2spay.org

Still have questions about spaying or neutering your dog? Check out this site.

A Simple Glossary

aggression A hostile reaction; self-defense in the face of a real or perceived threat. Aggression is the fight part of the "fight or flight" instinct.

allergies Dogs can have allergies, just as people can, and often to the same things.

alpha Behaviorists who study pack behavior in dogs and wolves call the top dog – the leader of the pack – the alpha dog.

American Kennel Club (AKC) An organization that registers purebred dogs and licenses dog shows and other dog sporting events.

body language Positions of the body, of body parts and facial expressions; dogs use canine body language to communicate.

bonding The deep commitment dog and owner feel for each other; that sense of responsibility for one another.

boundary training Teaching the puppy to remain behind you and to respect boundaries.

buckle collar A wide nylon, cotton, or leather collar that fastens with a buckle.

Buster Cube A plastic cube dog toy with an adjustable hole in one side so you can fill the cube with kibble. The dog must manipulate the cube to get the kibble out.

call name The name you call your dog every day.

choke collar A training collar that works with a snap and release motion.

come A command that requires the dog to stop everything and come directly to you.

conformation Competitive dog shows for evaluating a dog as compared to others of his breed and as compared to the breed standard.

correction A verbal or physical way of telling the dog he's made a mistake.

CPR An emergency first aid procedure to keep your dog's heart beating and to keep him breathing.

cue Command, signal.

distractions Things that can break the dog's concentration.

doggy door A flap that is installed in one of the doors to your house. It enables the dog to go from inside the house to the outside and back again without any assistance from you.

dominance Levels of hierarchy within the pack or family group.

fearful aggression A timid or shy dog reacting in an aggressive manner; aggression caused by fear.

fear period A crucial period in a puppy's development, during which the pup is particularly sensitive to scary objects and situations. Anything that scares the puppy now could become a lifelong fear.

force Making the dog do what you want; also, physical strength.

free feeding Leaving food out for your puppy to nibble on all day.

groomer A person whose career is caring for the skin and coat of dogs, cats, and other pets.

halter A training tool that fits over the dog's head, much like a horse's halter; used instead of a training collar.

heartworm A parasitic worm that lives in the heart; untreated, it causes death.

heel The dog walks by your left side, with his neck and shoulders even with your left leg.

hookworm An intestinal parasite.

housetraining Teaching the puppy to relieve himself outside, not in the house.

instinct Inborn urges to respond to things in a specific manner.

killed virus A type of vaccine in which the virus is dead, but it still stimulates the body to produce antibodies.

Kong A hard, hollow toy that looks like three rubber balls that have been squashed together.

leash awareness Teaching the puppy to be aware of the leash and owner; to respect the leash.

let's go A command used to teach the puppy to walk nicely on the leash without pulling.

long line A longer length of leash or clothesline rope, used as a training tool for the "come" command and for boundary training.

lure Something the dog will follow to be shaped into a position or to learn a command.

lure coursing Working evaluation for sighthounds.

mat A knotted tangle of hair. It's important to comb mats out before they get too tight. Otherwise, they work their way down to the dog's skin and can really hurt.

microchip A tiny transponder, no bigger than a grain of rice, that your vet injects under the skin near the shoulder. It is a permanent means of identification.

modified live virus A type of vaccine in which the virus is altered to decrease its virulence, but is still a live virus.

motivation Helping the dog want to do something; providing a reward.

motivator The reward for doing something right; the lure to do something right.

negative attention Attention with unpleasant consequences; some dogs will get into trouble simply for the attention, even negative attention.

neuter Castrating a male dog by removing the testicles through an incision just in front of the scrotum.

parasite An organism that lives off another.

pinch or prong collar A multi-link training collar that pinches when it is pulled.

positive reinforcement Anything positive: verbal praise, petting, food treats, toys.

praise Verbal affirmation, approval.

purebred Dogs whose parents, grandparents, and ancestors for several generations back were all of the same breed.

quick A bundle of nerves and bloods vessels inside the nail.

registered name The official name recorded with the organization where the dog is registered. Often it includes the kennel name of the breeder.

Rocky Mountain spotted fever A disease transmitted by ticks.

shock A life-threatening condition caused by a trauma.

sit A training position with the hips down and the front end up.

socialization Introducing the puppy to different people, sights, sounds, and smells.

spay A surgical ovariohysterectomy for a female dog. The ovaries and uterus are removed through an incision in the abdomen.

standard A written description of the breed, and describes a perfect dog of that breed by looks, physical conformation, how it moves, its temperament, and its working abilities.

stay A training command that means "hold the position without moving."

submissive Showing respect for dominance.

temperament Personality and character.

time-out A time away from training that gives the dog a chance to rest and think, and breaks the thought process, especially if the dog has been misbehaving.

tourniquet A device used to stop major blood flow after an injury.

vaccination Injections of a small amount of a specified disease that enables the body to develop antibodies to protect itself from the disease.

wait A training command that means "hold still and wait for another command."

Index

Acknowledgements

Publisher's acknowledgement

Dorling Kindersley would like to thank Valerie Buckingham and Sheema Mookherjee for editorial help.

Picture credit

Picture Researcher: Samantha Nunn
Picture Librarians: Richard Dabb and David Saldanha

The publisher would like to thank the following for their kind permission to reproduce their photographs: (Abbreviations key: t=top, b=bottom, r=right, l=left, c=centre)

Ardea London Ltd: 91b; John Daniels 90cr, 107cr, 125cr, 184tr, 188l, 190cr, 204b.
Bruce Coleman Ltd: Adriano Bacchella 8-9, 10-11, 220t; Jane Burton 170b.
Corbis: Charles Philip 50t.
Joe Cornish: 135cl.
The Image Bank/Getty Images: 26, 152.
FLPA - Images of nature: Foto Natura 250l; Roger Wilmshurst 241br.
Tracy Morgan: 5br, 7b, 24br, 29tr, 38br, 40br, 45cr, 47tr, 52tr, 64b, 67t, 84br, 86b, 93tl, 95tr, 98bl, 99tr, 101tr, 110cr, 117bl, 117bc, 121bc, 123bl, 124tr,
129bl, 132tr, 132tr, 139, 143br, 150bl, 150br, 154b, 162, 164bl, 195tr, 195br, 211br, 213br, 214cl, 215br, 228br, 239br, 240br, 247tr, 254cr, 254crb, 255cr, 256t, 260tr, 262, 264bc, 264bcl, 266b, 268br, 272br, 274br.
N.H.P.A.: B & C Alexander 48b.
Stephen Oliver: 76b, 77tr.
Oxford Scientific Films: Alan and Sandy Carey 36; Dale C. Spartas/Okapia 128.
The Photographers' Library: 97bl.
Powerstock Photolibrary / Zefa: 153b, 256b.
RSPCA: 66; Cheryl A. Ertelt 102, 270tr; Angela Hampton 80, 96cr, 100bl, 102tl, 202, 236, 249tr, 271br; E. A. Janes 32bl, 114l.
Corbis Stock Market: 90, 172; Tim Davis 83br; LWA/Dann Tardif 91tr.
Stone/Getty Images: 14l, 52l; Tim Davis 70t; Dale Durfee 131bl; Kathi Lamm 46tl; Renee Lynn 134t.
Superstock Ltd.: Kai Chiang 222.
Telegraph Colour Library/Getty Images: 2, 140; Arthur Tilley 94br, 259cr; V.C.L./Paul Viant 128tr.